An Orange Tree Thea
Stephen Joseph Theatre Sc
co-

NORTHANGER ABBEY

by ZOE COOPER from the novel by JANE AUSTEN

This play was first performed on 20 January 2024
at the Orange Tree Theatre, Richmond

CAST
Cath **Rebecca Banatvala**
Iz **AK Golding**
Hen **Sam Newton**

CREATIVES AND PRODUCTION TEAM
Writer **Zoe Cooper**
Director **Tessa Walker**
Designer **Hannah Sibai**
Lighting Designer **Matt Haskins**
Sound Designer and Composer **Holly Khan**
Movement Director **Jonnie Riordan**
Casting Director **Matilda James**
Costume Supervisor **Anna Dixon**
Production Electrician and Relighter **Gabriel Finn**
Dialect Coach **Deborah Garvey**
Assistant Director **Namoo Chae Lee**

Production Manager **Lisa Hood**
Company Stage Manager **Jenny Skivens**
Deputy Stage Manager/ CSM on book **Jeanette Maggs**
Assistant Stage Manager **Jamie Craker**
Production and rehearsal photography **Pamela Raith**

Thanks
Stuart Burgess and Priya Virdee
Lute supplied by The Lute Society, www.Lutesociety.org

3

REBECCA BANATVALA
Cath

Theatre credits include: *Sap* (Edinburgh Festival Fringe – Paines Plough Roundabout and Soho Theatre/UK tour); *I F*cked You In My Spaceship* (VAULT Festival); *Much Ado About Nothing* (RSC); *Mrs Puntila and her Man Matti* (Royal Lyceum Theatre); *Rotterdam* (UK tour); *The Three Musketeers* (The Dukes) and *Trident Moon* (Finborough Theatre).

Television credits include Series 2 of BBC Drama *Vigil*, *The Syndicate* (BBC), *Love, Death & Robots* (Netflix), and *Emmerdale* (ITV).

Film credits include *The Princess Switch 3* (Netflix).

Trained at Royal Central School of Speech and Drama.

AK GOLDING
Iz

Theatre credits include *Twelfth Night* (Nottingham Playhouse); *The Messiah Complex* (VAULT Festival); *Tapped* (UK tour); *Hot in Here: An Energy Generating Dance Party* (UK tour); *Move Fast and Break Things* (FREIGHT THEATRE, Edinburgh Fringe); *Extra Time* (Derby Theatre) and *Hamlet* (National Theatre).

Television credits include *Urban Myths: Handel and Hendrix*.

Film credits include *The Colour Room, Mantis* and *Silence*.

Trained at Bristol Old Vic Theatre School.

ZOE COOPER
Writer

Zoe Cooper's adaptation of David Almond's novel *A Song For Ella Grey* opens at Northern Stage, Newcastle, on 1st February 2024 before touring York Theatre Royal, Theatre Peckham, Hull Truck, Liverpool Playhouse and Yvonne Arnaud Theatre Guildford. It is produced by Pilot Theatre in association with Northern Stage and York Theatre Royal and directed by Esther Richardson. Her new play *The Cambium Layer* was shortlisted for the Women's Prize For Playwriting in December 2023.

Zoe Cooper's play *Out of Water* (Orange Tree Theatre/RSC) was shortlisted for the Charles Wintour Award for Most Promising Playwright at the Evening Standard Awards 2019, was a finalist for the Susan Smith Blackburn Award and nominated for the Best New Production of a Play Award in the Broadway World UK Awards. Her play *Jess and Joe Forever* (Orange Tree Theatre/national tour/Traverse Theatre) won the Most Promising Playwright Award at the Off West End Awards 2017 and was longlisted for the Evening Standard Most Promising Playwright Award. Her other plays include *The Kiss* (part of the Orange Tree Theatre's *Inside/Outside* collection of live streamed plays); *The Snow Queen* (National Theatre 'Let's Play' scheme); and *Nativities* and *Petrification* (Live Theatre).

Zoe studied as a playwright on the Royal Court Young Writers'

SAM NEWTON
Hen

Theatre credits include *A Woman Walks into a Bank* (Theatre503); *Big Big Sky* (Hampstead Theatre); *Sometimes Thinking* (Frantic Assembly); *The Curious Incident of the Dog in the Night-Time* (Piccadilly Theatre, UK and international tour); Nigel Slater's *Toast* (The Lowry, Edinburgh Festival Fringe); *Good Day* (VAULT Festival) and *Jack and the Beanstalk* (Jacksons Lane).

Television credits include *The Bastard Son and The Devil Himself*, *Newark, Newark* and *Casualty*.

Trained at Royal Central School of Speech and Drama.

Programme. She completed an MPhil in Playwriting at the University of Birmingham and completed her PhD at Newcastle University, where she also lectures on drama.

TESSA WALKER
Director

Recent productions include *Biscuits for Breakfast* (Hampstead Theatre); *Run, Rebel* (Pilot Theatre, tour); *Symphony of Us* (Coventry Cathedral, Coventry City of Culture) and *The Glad Game* (Nottingham Playhouse, Hampstead Theatre and on film).

She was Associate Director at Hampstead Theatre from 2021 – 2023 where she directed *Ravenscourt* and *Big, Big, Sky*. As Associate Director at Birmingham Repertory Theatre she directed *The Whip Hand, Looking for John, Folk, The Quiet House, Circles, Back Down, 366 Days of Kindness, How to be a Hero, Jekyll and Hyde, 101 Dalmatians, The Lion, the Witch and the Wardrobe, A Christmas Carol* and *The Mother.*

Other directing includes *The Gatekeeper* (Royal Exchange Theatre); *The Company Will Overlook a Moment of Madness* (National Theatre of Scotland); *Dream Pill, Dancing Bears* (Clean Break at Soho Theatre); *She From the Sea* (Clean Break at LIFT); *Harm's Way* (The Lowry, Manchester); *Black Crows* (Clean Break at Arcola Theatre); *Orange* (Script Cymru) and *Debris* (Theatre503, BAC Critics' Choice Season, Traverse Edinburgh and Staatstheater Biennale, Germany).

HANNAH SIBAI
Designer

Hannah is a British/Syrian theatre designer based in Yorkshire. She is particularly interested in designing performance spaces for new writing, devised, playful or interactive performances. She is a keen collaborator with directors, writers, composers and performers to create design-lead work from the earliest stages of development.

Selected Theatre Design credits: *Arabian Nights* (Bristol Old Vic); *A Play for the Living in a Time of Extinction* (Headlong, York Theatre Royal and Barbican); *24(Day)The Measure of my Dreams* (Almeida Theatre); *The Lost Spells* (Goblin, Polka, Watford Palace, Theatre by the Lake); *The City and the Town* (Riksteatern Sweden, Hull Theatre and Matthew Linley Creative Projects); *A Christmas Carol* (Shakespeare North); *The Doncastrian Chalk Circle* (National Theatre and Cast); *A Tale of Orpheus & Eurydice* (Opera North); *REGNANT* (HOME); *Love n Stuff* (Oldham Coliseum); *The Travelling Pantomime* (York Theatre Royal); *Two* (Gala Theatre); *Handbagged* (English Theatre Frankfurt); *Bassett* (Sheffield Crucible); *SET FIRE TO EVERYTHING!!!* (RashDash) and *Country Music* (Leeds Playhouse).

MATT HASKINS
Lighting Designer

Theatre credits include: *Peter Pan Goes Wrong* (Broadway/West End/Canada/Australia); *The Empress* (RSC); *Frankenstein* (UK tour); *Miss Saigon* (Folketeateret Oslo); *School Girls; Or, The African Mean Girls Play* (Lyric Hammersmith); *The City and The Town* (Hull Truck/Riksteatern Sweden); *Mary, Fever Syndrome, Biscuits for Breakfast, Ravenscourt* (Hampstead Theatre); *The Clinic* (Almeida Theatre); *Hakawatis* (Shakespeare's Globe); *Private Peaceful* (Nottingham Playhouse); *Fair Play* (Bush Theatre); *The Lovely Bones* (Birmingham Rep/UK tour); *Nina* (Young Vic/Unity Theatre). Matt lit the iconic Grace Jones at the Royal Albert Hall and was Associate Lighting Designer for *The Master* and *Margarita* (Complicité).

HOLLY KHAN
Sound Designer and Composer

Holly is a British/Guyanese composer, sound designer and multi-instrumentalist creating scores for theatre, film and installation.

Most recent theatre work includes: *A Child of Science* (Bristol Old Vic); the Olivier nominated *Blackout Songs, This Much I Know, Biscuits for Breakfast* (Hampstead Theatre); *Tess* (Turtle Key Arts/Sadler's Wells); *Dreaming and Drowning* (Bush Theatre); *I Really Do Think This Will Change Your Life* (Colchester Mercury); *Duck*

(Arcola Theatre); *The Invincibles* (Queen's Theatre Hornchurch); *Unseen Unheard* (Theatre Peckham); *Jules and Jim* (Jermyn Street Theatre); *Mansfield Park* (The Watermill Theatre); *The Beach House* (Park Theatre); *For A Palestinian* (Bristol Old Vic/Camden People's Theatre – OFFIE nominated for Best Sound Design); *Amal Meets Alice* (Good Chance Theatre Company, The Story Museum); *Kaleidoscope* (Filskit Theatre Company, Southbank Centre/Oxford Playhouse); *Ticker* (Alphabetti Theatre, Newcastle/Underbelly, Edinburgh/Theatre503).

Film and Installation work includes *Becoming An Artist: Bhajan Hunjan* (Tate Kids); *One Day* (Blind Summit Theatre, Anne Frank Trust); *Sanctuary* (Limbic Cinema, Stockton Arts Festival); *Song for the Metro* (The Sage Music Centre, Newcastle); *It's About Time* (UN Women/Battersea Arts Centre/Mayor of London); *Their Voices* (RAA and Global Health Film Festival, Barbican).

JONNIE RIORDAN
Movement Director

As Director: *Blood Harmony* and *PETRICHOR* (ThickSkin); *The Witchfinder's Sister* (Queens Theatre Hornchurch); *Eavesdropping* (ThickSkin, Traverse Theatre); Nigel Slater's *Toast* (West End, UK tour); *AWOL* (ThickSkin, Tron Theatre Glasgow) and *Boy Magnet* (ThickSkin, Theatr Clwyd).

As Movement Director: *Quiz* (Chichester/UK tour – Co Movement Director); *Cuckoo* (Royal Court Downstairs); *Hope has a Happy Meal* (Royal Court Upstairs); *The Book of Will* (Queens Theatre Hornchurch/Octagon Theatre Bolton/Shakespeare North Playhouse); *A Christmas Carol* (Octagon Theatre Bolton); *How Not to Drown* (ThickSkin, Traverse Theatre); *Great Apes* (Arcola Theatre); *Eyes closed, Ears covered* (The Bunker); *Maggie and Pierre* (Finborough Theatre); *Mobile* (The Paper Birds); *Home* (Frozen Light, UK tour); *Caught* (Pleasance Theatre) and *A Tale of Two Cities* (USF, Brit Project).

As Associate Director: *Things I Know to Be True* (Frantic Assembly, UK tour); *The Static* (ThickSkin, UK tour); *Chalk Farm* (ThickSkin, Bush Theatre, Off Broadway) and *Blackout* (ThickSkin).

As Associate Movement Director: *Whisper House* (The Other Palace) and *Myth* (RSC, Mischief Festival).

DEBORAH GARVEY
Dialect Coach

Deborah is a dialect, voice and singing coach. She is on the BA Acting Voice team at RADA and previously worked at Royal Central School of Speech and Drama teaching both voice and singing. She provides coaching support on RADA public productions and recent professional coaching credits include: *Henry V* (Donmar Warehouse); *Kraven the Hunter* (Sony Pictures); *Yellowman* (Orange Tree Theatre); *Be More Chill* (The Other Palace); *Brief Encounter* (The Watermill Theatre); *POT* (Ovalhouse) and *Ripped* (Tristan Bates Theatre).

NAMOO CHAE LEE
Assistant Director

Namoo is the Resident Assistant Director at the Orange Tree Theatre. Currently pursuing her MFA in Theatre Directing at Birkbeck College, UoL, *Northanger Abbey* is her second time assisting at the Orange Tree Theatre after the 2023 JMK Award-winning production of *Meetings*. Prior to that, she received her training as a musical theatre writer at Tisch School of Arts, NYU, and worked as a director and performer in the U.S. and South Korea. Her assisting credit includes *Yerma* (Rose Bruford); *Hamlet* (Colsubsidio Theater, Colombia); *The Lesson* (Foarte Mic Theatre, Romania); *Komachi Huden* (Shizuoka Performing Arts Park, Japan); *The Hour That We Knew Nothing About Each Other* (Uridongne Theatre, S. Korea); *Golden Dragon* (SFAC, S. Korea).

JEANETTE MAGGS
Deputy Stage Manager

Jeanette has a background in Sound, AV and Production Management for film, installations and theatre. She has been working in Company Stage Manager, Deputy Stage Manager and Assistant Stage Manager roles for the last ten years.

Recent credits include *Little Red Riding Hood* (The Rep, Birmingham 2023); *Not The Last* (Women And Theatre, Birmingham 2023); *Wind In The Willows* (The Garrick, Lichfield 2023); *Biscuits For Breakfast* (Hampstead Theatre, London 2023) and *Run Rebel* (Pilot Theatre, tour, 2023).

JAMIE CRAKER
Assistant Stage Manager

Jamie graduated from Bristol Old Vic Theatre School in Summer 2021 with an FdA in Production Arts for Stage. She has since worked as an Assistant Stage Manager, Deputy Stage Manager, props-maker and props-buyer. This is her third production at the Orange Tree Theatre, having previously worked on *Arms and the Man* (2022/23) and *The False Servant* (2022).

Her other theatre credits include: *The Seven Deaths of Maria Callas* (London Coliseum, 2023); *Peter Grimes* and *Iolanthe* (English National Opera, 2023); *Assassins, Woman in Mind, The Taxidermist's Daughter* (Chichester Festival Theatre); *The Nativity* (Wintershall and tour); *Maggie & Ted* (Yvonne Arnaud Theatre) and *Beauty and the Beast* (Disney Theatrical UK and Ireland tour, 2021).

ORANGE TREE THEATRE

A powerhouse of independent theatre

The Orange Tree (OT) is an award-winning, independent theatre. It is recognised as a powerhouse that creates high-quality productions of new and contemporary drama, revitalises classics and rediscoveries, and introduces children and young people to the magic of theatre.

The OT's home in Richmond, South West London, is an intimate theatre with the audience seated all around the stage: watching a performance here is truly a unique experience. We believe in the power of dramatic stories to entertain, thrill and challenge us; plays that enrich our lives by enhancing our understanding of ourselves and each other.

Founded by Sam Walters in 1971, the Orange Tree started life above the Orange Tree pub. It moved into the purpose-built in-the-round space it occupies today in 1991, adapted from a disused primary school. Over the last five decades the theatre has become known and loved for its policy of rediscovering lost gems and giving forgotten classics a new lease of life, as well as staging new works, developing relationships with writers such as Vaclav Havel and Martin Crimp,

and more recently, Zoe Cooper, Sonali Bhattacharyya and Joe White. The Orange Tree has collaborated with companies including the National Theatre and the RSC, and its work has been seen by thousands of people nationwide.

As a registered charity (266128) sitting at the heart of its community, we work with 10,000 people in Richmond and beyond through participatory theatre projects for people of all ages and abilities. Our mission is to enable audiences to experience the next generation of theatre talent, experiment with ground-breaking new drama and explore the plays from the past that inspire the theatre-makers of the present. Operating without regular support from Arts Council England, the OT relies on the support of its audiences and funders to raise £500k a year to create this outstanding work on stage and in the community.

Artistic Director and Joint CEO
Tom Littler
Executive Director and Joint CEO
Hanna Streeter

orangetreetheatre.co.uk

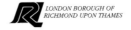

LONDON BOROUGH OF
RICHMOND UPON THAMES

At the Octagon Theatre in Bolton, we believe in the transformative power of theatre and the arts. Our mission is simple: to bring people together and enrich communities through the magic of storytelling and creativity. We want you to feel heard and cherished in a community that is full of Northern wit, warmth, and grit.

Our unique, intimate, and flexible auditorium is home to productions that are bold, adventurous and popular, putting audiences in the heart of the action – kindling collective joy and unforgettable experiences.

Our engagement programmes provide creative opportunities for all ages. We believe that everyone has their own story, and that theatre is an amazing tool for sparking and building the confidence of people to tell theirs.

We strive to make the world a brighter place through artistic expression and collaborating with our communities.

Join us at the Octagon — a place where magic happens, and stories come alive.

The Octagon is led by Chief Executive **Roddy Gauld** & Artistic Director **Lotte Wakeham**.

Winner, Manchester's Leading Arts and Cultural Venue 2023. Nominated, UK Theatre of the Year 2023.

The Octagon is a registered charity, number 248833.

FUNDERS

PRINCIPAL SPONSOR

PRINCIPAL PATRON

Sue Hodgkiss, CBE DL

SJT Stephen Joseph Theatre

The Stephen Joseph Theatre (SJT) is an independent producing theatre based in Scarborough, North Yorkshire.

Our home is a beautifully-restored 1930s Odeon cinema which houses our famous theatre-in-the-round, the first of its kind in the world, and the McCarthy, an end-on space for theatre and cinema.

We have provided world-class accessible theatre for audiences on the Yorkshire coast since 1955. We've produced over 700 plays, many of them new; developing new writers and writing was the primary aim of the company's founder, Stephen Joseph, and it remains a core part of our work today. Our regional, national and international reputation was historically pioneered by playwright and director Alan Ayckbourn (whose work continues to be premiered here) and it is now sustained and developed through a wide-ranging programme of high-quality theatre, film, music and comedy designed to offer audiences the broadest possible choice. For local audiences, and the thousands who visit this beautiful part of the world every year, SJT provides year-round entertainment: diverse, funny, surprising, visually daring and packing a big emotional punch.

Alongside the programme of work on our stages, we have an extensive participatory programme, working across the region and with all ages and communities: a youth theatre programme for anyone aged from 0 – 25; cross-generational dementia workshops which are acclaimed within the industry; schools' sessions and summer holiday activity. This work plays an increasingly important part of our civic role within the town and the county.

The SJT is led by Joint Chief Executives **Paul Robinson** (Artistic Director) and **Caroline Routh** (Executive Director).

The Stephen Joseph Theatre (as Scarborough Theatre Trust Ltd.) is a registered charity, number 253606.

THEATRE
by the
LAKE

Theatre by the Lake is Cumbria's professional producing theatre, bringing the world to Cumbria and Cumbria to the world.

Each year we produce work of acclaimed ambition and integrity, and present nearly 400 performances across our two auditoria. Theatre made by TBTL, in Cumbria, tours on a national scale as well as to communities across the region. We also present an eclectic programme of professional visiting work. At our home on the banks of Derwentwater, we welcome a mix of audiences from across Cumbria and those visiting The Lakes from across the globe.

We create opportunities for people of all ages and interests, from developing local artists to engaging young people in all aspects of what we do. We also host and support performances by local charities, community groups and amateur companies.

The theatre has been hailed by The Independent as 'the most beautifully located and friendly theatre in Britain' and is just a short stroll from Derwentwater on the edge of Keswick, amid the magnificent western fells of the Lake District, which has been awarded UNESCO World Heritage status.

From its origins as the Blue Box, Theatre by the Lake was willed into existence by the local community and opened by Dame Judi Dench in 1999. 25 years later, under the co-leadership of Artistic Director, Liz Stevenson and Executive Director, Simon Stephens, the theatre continues to consolidate its role as a vital community asset, embarking on a new strategic direction which places emphasis on our social value and an inherent connection to place.

Theatre by the Lake (as Cumbria Theatre Trust) is a registered charity, number 516673.

Supported using public funding by
ARTS COUNCIL ENGLAND

County Council

Keswick
Town Council

Writer's Note

'There seems almost a general wish of decrying the capacity and undervaluing the labour of the novelist.. "I am no novel-reader—I seldom look into novels—Do not imagine that I often read novels—It is really very well for a novel." Such is the common cant. "And what are you reading, Miss——?" "Oh! It is only a novel!" replies the young lady, while she lays down her book with affected indifference, or momentary shame. "It is only Cecilia, or Camilla, or Belinda..."'

Northanger Abbey by Jane Austen

I first read *Northanger Abbey* at nineteen, at roughly the same age Catherine Morland is when she goes to Bath. I was on my second attempt at going to University and I felt very out of place, awkward and grubby in the posh University town I found myself in. It had turrets and quads. It was full of people who knew which cutlery to use at a formal dinner and what a quad was. Who couldn't wait to go to actual balls and who had the right sort of frocks to wear to said actual balls. And who often said cutting things to me in tutorials which I only realised long after the event HAD been cutting, often while walking across what turned out to be a quad. And getting shooed off the grass.

I was there to read English Literature and the books we were tasked with debating in those tutorials were generally very male, very white, and very heterosexual, and also, not unrelatedly, Very Important. I'm actually not quite sure how *Northanger Abbey* made it onto one of those reading lists printed on orange paper and shoved into what I found out were called pigeonholes. Perhaps we grazed past Austen on our way to other maler, more Important writers. I do have a vague memory of someone in a gown lecturing us on how it was a satire on (silly female) gothic novels. And that was why it was quite clever. Although, I am sure he went on to say, not as clever as if it had been written by and was about men.

But in any case, I felt instantly at home in that weird, lumpy gothic first novel. It was about a girl who loved books and had a big imagination and whose love of books and imagining brought her to a city where she felt out of place and awkward and othered. But also over excited and often quite badly behaved. And latterly, how that same imagination got her into lots of quite cringey and awkward scrapes which were a bit spooky. But not too spooky, thank-goodness, as I was (and am) very much a scaredy cat and was dodging reading anything properly gothic or spooky at the time – not good to have to walk past turrets after reading about ghosts.

I liked that the very flawed heroine was a bookworm who thought herself into a series of fictional realities. How those fictional realities started to fight actual reality (reality-reality, if you will...). It reminded me of how I used to love being devoured by books before I learned to debate them. How I was able to live inside them. As Catherine says of a book at one point '"Oh! I am delighted with the book! I should like to spend my whole life in reading it. I assure you, if it had not been to meet you, I would not have come away from it for all the world."'

There was another reason I liked it too and that reason was a bit more secret. It felt a little bit naughty: It had a friendship in it I thought I recognised. The passages that described the quick and quickly growing friendship between Catherine and Isabella felt familiar:

'Here Catherine and Isabella, arm in arm, again tasted the sweets of friendship in an unreserved conversation; – they talked much, and with much enjoyment...They passed so rapidly through every gradation of increasing tenderness, that there was shortly no fresh proof of it to be given to their friends or themselves. They called each other by their Christian names.'

At one point another (rival?) friend is described by Isabella as:

'"...netting herself the sweetest cloak you can conceive. I think her as beautiful as an angel, and I am so vexed with the men for not admiring her! I scold them all amazingly about it!...Yes, that I do. There is nothing I would not do for those people who are really my friends. I have no notion of loving people by halves, it is not in my nature. My attachments are always excessively strong."'

And finally, that moment in all normal platonic friendship when one friend exclaims to the other:

'"I am determined at all events to be dressed exactly like you."'

In contrast the relationship between Catherine and Henry felt less romantic to me, less charged, less hormonal, although still full of love. The sadness in Henry and the strangeness of his knowing a lot about women's dresses and being very close to his sister interested me. It felt and feels like an echo of the sort of friendship that can exist today between a mouthy messy woman and a gentle man...but which is rarely to be found between the covers of books or in films or TV shows for that matter.

I do think that a lot of queer readers will have had versions of this experience of reading. The moments when we think we have found versions of ourselves in texts we have been excluded from, either by the writer, or (more often) by other readers who tell us how to read those books, what is there and what most definitely is not.

I am thirty-nine now, I'm married to a woman and I am a mother myself. And I find myself sometimes tasked with standing in front of students, telling them what to think about books and plays. What is to be found there and what is not. And my relationship with Catherine Morland has changed. I feel very protective of her, and the mistakes she makes. The person I think she is. But it still feels a bit naughty to be able to see those versions of myself and my friends at nineteen and twenty in this now widely accepted Very Important writer's work. I am delighted that Jane has made her way very belatedly into the literary canon, but she must feel quite wobbly about being there and I feel wary of doing anything that might draw attention to the otherness I find in her writing. The bits of her that don't quite seem to fit the narratives people have created around her and for her.

However, I think the permission to find those other stories in her books is in what she writes. At one point Catherine dismisses books of history:

'"I read it a little as a duty, but it tells me nothing that does not either vex or weary me. The quarrels of popes and kings, with wars or pestilences, in every page; the men all so good for nothing, and hardly any women at all—it is very tiresome: and yet I often think it odd that it should be so dull, for a great deal of it must be invention. The speeches that are put into the heroes' mouths, their thoughts and designs—the chief of all this must be invention, and invention is what delights me in other books"'

Northanger Abbey is absolutely a book about invention. It revels in layers of fictionality, of imagination. I have loved spending time in it again. I will have a hard time leaving it.

Zoe Cooper, December 2023.

Zoe Cooper would like to thank:

Lorne Campbell
Emily Cooper
James Harriman Smith
Guy Jones
Aoife Kennan
Jonathan Kinnersley
Tom Littler
Jodie McNee
Sid Sagar
Tom Wells
Emma Whipday

As always Marie Stern-Peltz.

And especially Tessa Walker.
Tessa, you made this process so delightful. It has been
a dream to finally work with you. Thank you so much.

NORTHANGER ABBEY

Zoe Cooper

After the book by Jane Austen

Characters

CATH, *female*
IZ, *female*
HEN, *male*

A Note About the Way that Character Works in this Story

Cath, Hen and Iz were in their late teens or early twenties when the events in Bath and at Northanger Abbey took place.

They are probably not much older than that when they retell their story.

In telling their story they play all the other characters. They also frequently swap roles, take over from each other, contradicting the telling.

A Note on How Dialogue is Set Out in the Script

When characters are telling the story, or talking between themselves in the present, speech is set out without speech marks, like this:

    CATH. And in this part I am with my parents.

When a character is speaking to another character in the past, in the story, it is set out with speech marks around the dialogue, like this:

    CATH. 'Mr Mullen says I have to practise, if I am to entertain our guests.'

Sometimes a character will swap modes within a single bit of dialogue. Like this:

> CATH. But the point of this part is that I did, on the eve of the anniversary of my previously established violent and dangerous entry into the world, announce a demonstration of '…all three of my aforementioned skills together in a grand concert, tomorrow on the occasion of my fourteenth birthday…'

As mentioned, sometimes the characters will play other roles in the story. Character names will be set out with the role they are playing following their own name. Like this:

> HEN/MAM. 'That will do extremely well, our Cath.'

A Note on Text

A forward slash (/) indicates the point at which a speaker is interrupted.

Words in square brackets indicate what is implied but not spoken.

Words in dialogue which are in brackets but not in italics are meant as asides spoken to the audience.

This text went to press before the end of rehearsals and so may differ slightly from the play as performed.

Prologue

Pre-set: CATH *and* IZ *are in the space as the audience enter.*

While they wait for everyone to make themselves comfortable,
IZ *is trying on some moustaches and sideburns. Maybe she*
keeps them all in a book, carefully pressed. Maybe she checks
the effect of each in a little mirror. At first she does so quietly.
But as time goes on, maybe she gets a bit bored and starts being
a bit silly. Trying to make members of the audience laugh.

CATH *does not approve of this.*

IZ *tries on an especially silly moustache.*

CATH. Iz.

IZ. What, Cath?

CATH. Put / them [away].

IZ (*silly voice*). What? Do you not like my / moustaches…

　　CATH *tries not to laugh.* HEN *enters, carrying props* CATH
　　has instructed him to bring. She checks what he has against
　　a list. Bosses him about, telling him to bring more, take
　　others away again, etc., etc.

　　It's nearly time. HEN *starts to put on a pinny.*

　　That is my…

CATH. She is right.

HEN. Then what am I to / wear…

　　CATH *holds up a dress/bump for* HEN. *He puts it on.*
　　Meanwhile IZ *puts the pinny on.*

　　They all agree that they are almost ready to begin. They
　　indicate this to stage management.

HEN *looks up at* IZ, *indicates the moustache she is still wearing.*

IZ. What?

CATH *sees. Indicates to* IZ, *who pulls it off.*

CATH. You must concentrate. Both of you. We are about to…

Lighting change.

(*To the audience.*) *Northanger Abbey.*

Act One, Scene One.

My birth.

Another lighting change.

ACT ONE

Scene One

The Birth of an Heroine

HEN/MAM *is on all-fours, on a bed*.

HEN/MAM. '…aarrrrrrrrr…'

IZ/MIDWIFE. 'That's it, Mrs M.'

HEN/MAM. '…ghhhhhhh…'

IZ/MIDWIFE (*simultaneous*). 'You know what to do.'

HEN/MAM (*simultaneous*). '…GGHHHHHHHHHHHHHH…'

IZ/MIDWIFE. 'You're an old hand at this after all, aren't you.'

HEN/MAM. 'AAARGGHHHHHHHHHH…'

IZ/MIDWIFE. 'So you just take all that pain and push it / down.'

HEN/MAM (*ragefully, in* IZ/MIDWIFE*'s face*).
    'GARGHHHHHHHHH… '

IZ/MIDWIFE (*raising her voice to be heard over* HEN/MAM*'s
    scream*).…'PUSH IT RIGHT DOWN INTO YOUR BUM.'

HEN/MAM *stops screaming*.

HEN/MAM*'s contraction has finished*.

HEN/MAM *pants*.

IZ/MIDWIFE *tries to mop* HEN/MAM*'s brow with a bit of
old muslin*.

HEN/MAM *bats her hand away, annoyed by this pointless
gesture*.

Through the following, IZ/MIDWIFE *tries to help* HEN/MAM
*as she makes her way painstakingly to a chamber pot and
wees*.

HEN. Because it starts with a plain mother.

CATH. At the end of a very long, quite *terrible* labour that could very well have killed her.

IZ. But which won't.

CATH. Leaving the poor child / motherless.

HEN. Which didn't.

IZ. Kill anyone we mean.

HEN. On account of the plain mother's unusually strong constitution.

HEN/MAM has finished weeing and is making her way back to the bed.

IZ. And also on account of the attendant midwife, a no-fuss least-said-soonest-mended salt-of-the-earth sort of person, from the village.

HEN/MAM is back at the bed, leaning on it.

IZ/MIDWIFE is in the process of having a look up her skirts. She breaks off to add:

Whose name was Peg, as it goes. (*As* IZ/MIDWIFE, *looking up* HEN/MAM*'s skirts.*) 'It's the size of the head.'

HEN/MAM starts to have another contraction.

HEN/MAM. 'Ohhhhhhhhh…'

IZ/MIDWIFE. 'It's just, well, sorry to say, Mrs M, but really exceptionally bloody massive.'

HEN/MAM. 'AHHHHHHHHHHHHHH!'

HEN/MAM's contraction reaches its peak. She goes silent. This is the worst pain she has experienced so far.

HEN/MAM pants through the following:

CATH. And even though this baby is being born to a plain mother and in a plain room like we have explained…

IZ.…and being number three of eight can hardly be considered an auspicious position…

CATH....*nevertheless...*

Another contraction begins.

HEN/MAM *does a long guttural groan.*

HEN, IZ *and* CATH. 'Pop!'

IZ/MIDWIFE. 'Now that huge great bonce is out, that's the hard part over with. One final push, Mrs M. Give it some welly!'

IZ, HEN *and* CATH *make a flopping-slippery-birth noise, they enjoy it even more than their head-popping noise.*

IZ/MIDWIFE *is clamping and cutting the umbilical cord and vigorously wiping down the baby through the following:*

'There we are. All done! Oh look at him.'

CATH *and* HEN/MAM. 'A boy?!'

IZ/MIDWIFE. 'It must be a boy...'

CATH. No, it can't be because we are doing my / birth.

IZ/MIDWIFE. 'Being so exceptionally... bonny...'

CATH (*warningly*). Isabella –

IZ/MIDWIFE. 'Oh, no, my mistake... It's a girl after all. It's just I assumed it was a boy at first, cos you did only ever produce lads, didn't you, Mrs M... and also because she is so... like I said, Mrs M... absolutely exceptionally bloody massive, / huge all over, isn't she?'

CATH *interrupts* IZ/MIDWFE *urgently, to stop her speaking.*

CATH. 'Waaaaa... waaaaa...'

IZ/MIDWIFE *wipes her hand across her forehead. Leaving a bloody streak.*

All three look at the baby.

Despite themselves, they are in awe.

HEN/MAM. 'My little Cath.'

CATH. And so, because from these humble...

IZ.…And ordinary and unremarkable…

CATH.…beginnings no one could have supposed *Catherine* Morland to be born An Heroine…

Scene Two

The Education of an Heroine

CATH *starts to play a lute*.

HEN/MAM. 'That's… a very… emphatic…'

IZ/PA (*muttering*). 'Emphatically tuneless…'

HEN. Muttered Cath's father.

IZ/PA (*snorting with laughter at his own joke; simultaneous*). 'Ha!'

HEN/MAM *and* CATH (*simultaneous*). 'Pa!'

HEN/MAM. 'A very *rousing* tune you are playing there, our Cath.'

CATH. Because this next scene takes place almost exactly fourteen years later…

IZ. Up a dirt track, near an unremarkable village, in a northern county of this country. In the same plain house which was…

HEN.…actually and in fact…

IZ.…a plain vicarage.

HEN. Not a very old vicarage.

IZ. Nor a very mysterious or very haunted vicarage.

HEN. But instead…

IZ. And in common with all its residents…

HEN.…an unremarkably plain vicarage…

CATH. And in this part I am with my parents.

IZ. Cath's plain mother, who you have already met...

HEN. ...and her father, like we have explained, who was, perhaps you guessed, a man of the church...

CATH (*regretfully*). And in common with his home and wife also plain.

IZ. ...And worse...

CATH (*even more regretfully*). Named Richard...

IZ/PA continues to visibly not enjoy CATH's playing.

'Mr Mullen...'

HEN. (...the Morland's long-suffering music teacher...)

CATH. '...says I have to practise, if I am to entertain our guests.'

IZ/PA (*to HEN/MAM, mildly alarmed*). 'Guests? What guests, Mam?'

HEN. Because as well as learning to play the lute, Cath had also, by this age, learned to sing in a tremulous voice...

CATH starts to sing in English.

And to speak French.

CATH starts to sing in French.

It is something operatic with a lot of emotion, which CATH really leans into.

And indeed to sing in such a romantically French voice that should she have needed to, our heroine was confident she could very well have distracted a dangerous criminal, in order that Cath could persuade this dangerous, murderous criminal who might indeed be generally foreign or specifically French, against his terrible purpose in coming to her home...

IZ. Because along with all three of her aforementioned talents...

CATH breaks off to add:

CATH. ...Everything we have already mentioned that I had already achieved by this still tender age...

CATH continues singing until...

HEN.…and above all that, Cath was already by this time…

CATH, IZ *and* HEN.…a girl of quite impressive imagination…

IZ/PA. 'Mam! What guests?! Because we never do…we don't ever have guests, do we, Mam?'

HEN/MAM. 'Oh! She only means the Allans, Pa.'

IZ/PA (*relieved*). 'Oh, the Allans.' (*To* CATH.) 'They aren't guests!'

CATH. 'Pfffff…'

IZ/PA. 'Thank goodness for that. I thought I should have to speak to new people!'

HEN. The Allans were a childless couple.

IZ/PA. 'Lucky buggers.'

HEN/MAM *and* CATH. 'Papa!'

IZ. Who were cut from the same plain cloth as Mam and Pa.

HEN. And who lived five fields away, in a house that was not a vicarage.

CATH. And which was a deal grander and a deal…

HEN. Well, slightly…

CATH.…A *deal* older.

HEN. And unfortunately it did indeed look like they were very likely to be the only people to enjoy…

IZ/PA. 'Endure! Endure eh, eh, Mam!'

CATH. '…the fruits of these, my not insignificant labours…'

HEN/MAM (*trying to thwack* IZ/PA *and trying not to laugh*). 'You naughty man!!'

CATH. But the point of this part is that I did, on the eve of the anniversary of my previously established *violent* and *dangerous* entry into the world, announce a demonstration of '…all three of my aforementioned skills together in a grand concert, tomorrow on the occasion of my fourteenth birthday to which you all, Mother, Father, my seven siblings, the Allans and Mr Mullan, most cordially welcomed' and *actually* all who attended admitted it to be a great success. The opera concert and its culminating aria being especially…

CATH *opens her mouth to sing once again…*

HEN/MAM. 'That will do extremely well, our Cath.'

IZ/PA. 'You have affected us long enough.'

HEN. It was shortly after this that Mr Mullan…

CATH. The last of the tutors to the Morland family…

IZ. In common with those poor unfortunates who came before him…

HEN. Decided that his talents…

CATH. Such as *they* were…

HEN. Were better exercised elsewhere.

CATH. And it must be admitted that the day that the frankly insufficient and somewhat incompetent music master was dismissed turned out to be one of the happiest days of my short life.

IZ. It must also be admitted that it was one of the happiest days of the Morlands' lives too.

HEN. As Mr Mullan was persuaded to take his lute with him.

HEN *takes the lute from* CATH.

Scene Three

The Miseducation of an Heroine

IZ/NIGEL *and* CATH *run up an incline. They are barefoot and dishevelled.*

CATH. The top of a grassy verge.

IZ. A little while later…

CATH. 'Unfortunately Grendel's mother is a girl.'

IZ. Because since Mr Mullan's departure Cath and her siblings had been staging a variety of selections from the great chronicles and stories.

CATH. 'She is a girl and so it is me that has to play her in this part.'

IZ/NIGEL *does a whine in response to this…*

IZ/NIGEL. 'Ohhhhhhh.'

CATH. Because being stuck in a northern county of this country and now without any sort of tutor, we were forced to provide our own education.

IZ/NIGEL. 'Because so far you have played the roles of Guinevere, King Arthur, Sir Gawain, and Beowulf, the monster Grendel, Hrothgar King of the Danes, Noah and Jonah and his whale.'

CATH. And in this moment I am about to give my Grendel's mother, the most fearsome of all. But Nigel…

IZ. Fifth youngest of Cath's brothers…

CATH. And quite the most trying, is being obstinate about things, as usual…

IZ/NIGEL. 'Because I said that I would be doing Grendel's ma's speech in this part.'

CATH. 'But…' I remind him, '…you have played Unnamed Criminal-Faced Manservant in the last three chronicles that we have enacted and in the great story we are doing today I am relying on you to reprise that important role…'

IZ/NIGEL. 'It is / not.'

CATH. 'And because he does need to reach his bloody end now, and in this story, so unfortunately we do not have time to discuss it.'

IZ/NIGEL. 'It's not / *fair*.'

CATH (*as* GRENDEL'S MOTHER, *in a patchy Danish/ Norwegian/Swedish accent. Perhaps it is oddly Dutch*). 'Oh, Criminal-Faced Manservant, you have been sent here to slay I, mother of Grendel and most fearsome monster of all of these lands. Did you think that you, only a puny, pimply…'

IZ/NIGEL. 'Oi!'

CATH (*as* GRENDEL'S MOTHER). '…and pathetic person with a face like that could ever hope to do as your master bid you?!'

IZ/NIGEL (*as* UNNAMED SERVANT). 'No I, I mean yes, because I am actually also very / [fearsome myself]!'

CATH (*as* GRENDEL'S MOTHER). 'Hararaggggggg…'

CATH/GRENDEL'S MOTHER *wrestles* IZ/NIGEL/ UNNAMED SERVANT *to the ground, they both roll down the grassy verge, giggling/wrestling. They stand up. Still giggling. But then* IZ/NIGEL *suddenly stops. He stares in horror at the back of* CATH'*s skirts. Then he starts to laugh again.*

IZ/NIGEL. 'Ha ha ha ha…'

CATH. 'When you laugh you open your mouth too wide and we can all see your terrible teeth.'

IZ/NIGEL *is still laughing.*

'And when you roar with your own amusement your face becomes so contorted that you appear like a…
Like the spectral horseman.'

IZ/NIGEL *carries on laughing.*

'Moan and yell loud at the lone hour of midnight…'

IZ/NIGEL *carries on laughing so that* CATH *has to raise her voice:*

IZ/NIGEL. 'Oh, Cath. What terrible offal...'

IZ/NIGEL *doubles over,* CATH *screams the last bit in his face.*

CATH. 'Then you shake from your skeleton folds the nightmares
Who,' *Nigel*, 'shrieking in agony, seek the couch
Of some fevered wretch who courts sleep in vain...'

CATH *has finished. She is very pleased with herself.*

IZ/NIGEL *is still laughing, wiping tears from his eyes, etc.*

IZ/NIGEL. 'I expect you got that off one of your precious poets, did you.'

CATH. 'It was created by myself, Nigel.'

IZ/NIGEL. 'Keats, was it?'

CATH. 'Most especially for you, Nigel.'

IZ/NIGEL. 'Or Shelley?'

CATH *looks shifty. It was Shelley.*

CATH. 'What is it anyway, Nigel? What is so very amusing?'

IZ/NIGEL. 'Your skirts.'

CATH *tries to turn to see. We see that there is a big bloody patch on the back of her skirts at the same time she does. She is having her first period.*

CATH (*partly to herself*). 'I... I... it can't be... it can't be yet, can it, Nigel? Because I thought I had...'

IZ/NIGEL. 'What?'

CATH. 'A few more.'

IZ. You thought you had a little more time.

CATH. Before the end of this part. But then my brother says: 'You will have to change...'

IZ/NIGEL. 'You will have to change how you behave now, won't you. Because real-life women don't roll down hills or take the part of Grendel's ma which I especially said I wanted to play. Real-life women cannot have any sorts of adventures and must only be sensible… and subservient…'

CATH. Which is a word that Nigel had only recently learnt from *Doctor Johnson's Dictionary of the English Language…*

IZ/NIGEL *leaves, singing.*

IZ/NIGEL. 'Subservient, subservient…'

CATH.…but which he very much enjoyed the sound of…

IZ/NIGEL. '…subservienttttttt…'

Scene Four

An Heroine Retreats

CATH *sits down.*

HEN. Catherine retreated after the incident on the grassy verge, into the house and onto the seat furthest away from the draught. She curled her feet under and drank ginger tea to stave off the pains.

CATH *opens a book.*

CATH. And I read.

Time passes.

A clock ticks.

Outside it is mizzling.

HEN/MAM *is pregnant again and folding laundry.*

IZ/PA. 'Cath.'

CATH (*not looking up*). 'Mmmm?'

IZ/PA. 'You have not been up these last five hours.'

CATH *ignores him.*

HEN/MAM. 'Don't you want to join your brothers?'

CATH (*still not looking up*). 'Pfff.'

IZ/PA (*looking out of a window*). 'They are playing another of your games of the imagination I think.'

HEN/MAM. '…down in the river.'

CATH. 'They will be doing Grendel's ma hiding in the lake.'

HEN/MAM (*mildly alarmed*). 'Nigel is standing atop little Phillip.'

CATH. 'Beowulf will dive deep into the lake and when he is right at the very bottom she will then hold him down.'

HEN/MAM (*slightly more alarmed*). 'Phillip is lying quite still in the water.'

CATH. 'Until he is almost completely lifeless.'

IZ/PA. 'Don't you want to join them?'

Beat.

CATH *does, but she doesn't want to admit it.*

CATH (*not looking up*). It is mizzling.'

Pause. IZ/PA *and* HEN/MAM *continue to watch the progress of the brothers outside.*

HEN/MAM. 'Ah good. Phillip is making his way out of the mud and so has not been drowned…'

IZ/PA. 'Or if you don't want to go without, to play with your brothers…'

HEN/MAM. '…That is a relief at least.'

IZ/PA. '…Perhaps the time has come for you to start helping your mam within, with some of her housewifely chores.'

CATH. 'Pfff…'

IZ/PA. 'I am sure that she would welcome your assistance, especially as she is with child…'

IZ/PA (*simultaneous*). '…Again.'

CATH (*under her breath, simultaneous*). 'Again…'

> (*To* IZ/PA *and* HEN/MAM.) 'Well. But unfortunately as you can see, I am indisposed, Father.'

IZ/PA. '"Indisposed" indeed…'

CATH (*sighing*). 'Because aside from my current condition of feminine indisposition, most unfortunately I find that there is very little outside our home or within it that interests me, Father.'

IZ/PA. 'Harrumph!'

CATH. 'Fiction is my only consolation against this, my most humdrum life.'

HEN. Because as you might have already surmised, Catherine had previously been something of an indiscriminate a reader.

IZ. But now she read only one kind of book.

HEN. The kind available for purchase in shops up and down this land.

CATH. 'In any case I have travelled quite a long way since I sat down.'

HEN. With lurid covers and costing only a very few pence.

CATH. 'All over France.'

IZ/PA. 'Eh?'

CATH. 'As far as the Mediterranean coast.'

HEN. The kind beloved by hordes of giggling young women of precisely Catherine's age, class and… condition, which allowed them to be transported to a variety of wrecked cathedrals, forlorn seascapes and haunted religious buildings.

CATH. 'Only yesterday I made the perilous journey with Emily St Aubert and her father across the Pyrenees…'

IZ/PA. 'Oh I see. You travel in your mind in these novels of yours. Very droll.'

CATH. '*The Mysteries of Udolpho* is more than a novel, Father.'

IZ/PA. 'You will begin to get sores. Your mother is six months gone, and yet she is more active than you. Just because you are having your first monthly...'

CATH *and* HEN/MAM. 'Pa!'

HEN/MAM (*whispering to* IZ/PA). 'You might be better not to say anything on these delicate matters which pertain to the female condition.'

IZ/PA *gives up, exits.*

Time passes.

HEN/MAM *is a little more pregnant again. She is mopping the floor, she pushes a sheepish* IZ/NIGEL *in front of her. He stands in front of* CATH *for a moment, not wanting to say what he has been told to say.*

'Cath.'

CATH (*reading*). 'Emily St Aubert has fallen hopelessly in love with the mysterious mystical Valancourt. He is quite the best hero I have ever read – '

HEN/MAM. 'Your brother has something to say.'

IZ/NIGEL. 'We have finished our game. And we have decided that you may come and choose the next.'

This is not all he has been told he has to say. He looks at HEN/MAM *who looks back: 'Say the next bit.' He steels himself.*

'And I am sorry, I should not have said the things I said about your... skirts. Or about ladies not having adventures.'

CATH (*not looking up*). 'Why?'

IZ/NIGEL. 'What?'

CATH (*still not looking up*). 'Why shouldn't you have said those things?'

IZ/NIGEL. 'Because Mam said I shouldn't have. (*Quickly, he knows he is not meant to say this bit to* CATH, *but can't help it*.) And-Pa-says-that-I-am-not-to-be-allowed-to-keep-my-rats-if-I-do-not-make-a-pretty-apology-and-you-do-not-get-up-off-your-behind.'

IZ/NIGEL *looks at* HEN/MAM *and shrugs. He tried his best. He is leaving, when…*

CATH. '"Emily gazed long on the splendours of the world she was quitting, of which the whole magnificence seemed thus given to her sight only to increase her regret on leaving it; for her, Valancourt alone was in that world; to him alone her heart turned, and for him alone fell her bitter tears."'

IZ/NIGEL. 'Sounds like a right soppy / twat.'

HEN/MAM. 'Nigel!'

CATH. 'These men of fiction, in all their complexity, are so much more interesting to me than the brothers in my life who are all so ignorant and impudent and… and… and with terrible terrible teeth!'

Time passes.

The clock sounds the hour.

HEN/MAM *is very very pregnant. She is holding a basket and a saw.*

IZ/PA. 'Would you not like to practise one of your poems for the Allans who are to visit?'

CATH. 'And what would be the object of my poetry, Pa? Emily St Aubert is now orphaned and her love affair with Valancourt is in danger because of the terrible Madame Cheron, an aunt who cares for her not a bit.'

HEN/MAM. 'You love your Aunt Allan.'

HEN/MAM *has a pain. She adjusts herself awkwardly.*

IZ/PA. 'Are you all right. Mam…'

HEN/MAM. 'It is probably just another practice pain, Pa…'

CATH. '…and who wants her to be forced into an unloving marriage with the dreadful Morano…'

HEN/MAM. '...do not fuss. Anyway, they are still quite far apart.'

CATH. '...And live in the terrible Castle of Udolpho.'

HEN/MAM. 'Although we should probably send for Peg.'

CATH. 'Although actually I think I would quite like to live in a castle.'

HEN/MAM. 'Just to be on the safe side.'

CATH. 'Especially if it were a very especially cursed sort of castle with lots of lovely turrets and battlements for throwing people over.'

HEN/MAM. 'I just need to pop up the ladder rested on the largest cherry tree and pick all the cherries for the jam and then do some quick coppicing of the other trees with this saw and then I shall have the baby... (*The pain becomes worse.*) Aaaaghhhhhhhh...'

CATH (*suddenly worried*). 'Mam...'

IZ/PA (*shouting off*). 'Nigel! Nigel! Where has that boy got to? Cath, go and find your brother and tell him he needs to run to the village to fetch Peg. You will have start boiling the hot water and preparing the muslin cloths.'

CATH. 'Me?!... But, Pa, I don't know what to / do...'

IZ/PA. 'Peg will be here as fast as she can but you know how quickly the babies have come these last three times. You have seen what has to be done, and you are old enough now to understand your proper place.'

CATH. 'My proper place?!'

IZ/PA. 'Please, Cath.'

HEN/MAM *makes an involuntary noise.*

CATH *exits.*

Time passes.

IZ/PA *and* HEN/MAM *have gone.*

CATH *returns. She looks done in. She sits down in the exact same spot she was in before. Opens the book. IZ/PA enters. He looks done in too. Maybe he has baby sick down him and is holding a big pile of soiled muslins, looking a bit dazed.*

'Your mam is still tired.'

Beat.

'Worn out from the birth…'

CATH. '*Yet another* birth you mean. Like a brood mare – '

IZ/PA. '…And you know very well that I do not like to… but I do… have to ask…?'

CATH. 'Ask what?

IZ/PA. 'Well.'

CATH. 'To ask me to help with my "proper" duties, as is my "proper" place, I expect? To boil the cherry jam and attend to my too-too-numerous siblings. To wipe the arses of my younger brothers, hold them when they are sick and spoon mush into their mouths when they are hungry and to assist with the scrubbing and washing and the mangle on a Sunday.'

IZ/PA. 'Cath…'

CATH. 'Just as all the other girls round here are asked to do. Sooner or later. Preparing me to meet a boy from a similar family not thirty miles from here and be married under that exact same cherry tree and put to breeding in the exact same way my mam was when she was matched with you.

That is simply the way of this world.'

Scene Five

An Heroine Must Go Out into the World

CATH. And so, on my seventeenth birthday, I finally rose from the chaise in the drawing room, no longer a child…

IZ. …But not yet a full lady…

CATH. …And made my speech:

'Father. Mother. I have come to understand that this northerly part of England is too small. Too narrow. Your company, though very sweet, is too plain, unremarkable and ordinary. Nothing of any consequence has ever happened or will ever happen to me while I am here. I must leave. I must enter society. You will have noticed that I have taken to curling my hair and I must now inform you that in common with all young heroines of my age, I find myself longing for balls.'

IZ/PA *sniggers,* HEN/MAM *elbows him to stop.*

HEN/MAM (*clutching herself*). 'Stoppit, Pa, you know I must be cautious of laughing too much ever since the arrival into the world of Cath's big head!'

CATH. And so it was decided I would accompany the Allans on their annual journey to the south and to Bath.

IZ. Mr Allan made the annual trip for the sake of his rheumatics. And everything indeed relative to this important journey was done on the part of the Morlands with a degree of moderation and composure which seemed more consistent with the common feelings of common life, than with the tender emotions a first separation of a heroine from her family ought always to excite. Cath's mam did offer some parting words of feminine advice.

HEN/MAM. 'Wrap yourself up very warm, try to keep some account of the money you spend…'

Frustrated by this humdrum advice, CATH *turns to go.*

IZ. And in her final statement…

HEN. A comment that would turn out to be bordering on the perceptive: (*As* MAM.) '...and, Cath, just...'

CATH *turns back, perhaps this advice will be more fitting for a romantic heroine...*

'Try to be kind to others and to yourself too, as we have always taught you.'

ACT TWO

Scene One

A Torrid Journey

HEN *is eager to play* MRS ALLAN. *He seizes the relevant piece of costume before* IZ *has a chance. All three sit down simultaneously in the carriage. It is a tight squeeze.*

The regular trot of hooves.

IZ. And so this is how Cath found herself inside the plain cloth-covered carriage, behind the two rather brown horses that the Allans always used.

HEN/MRS ALLAN. 'Oh it has begun to drip.'

IZ. Declared Mrs Allan.

HEN. Or Aunt Allan as she was known to young Cath.

HEN/MRS ALLAN *hands out travel sweets from a tin.*

CATH. 'And look at the clouds brewing with portent! I do hope that we will not be caught in a dreadful storm out on the moors…'

HEN/MRS ALLAN (*to* IZ/MR ALLAN). 'But it's just ordinary fields…'

CATH. 'And an old woman in rags stepping out in front…'

HEN/MRS ALLAN. 'What old woman?'

CATH. 'Causing the horses to fright.'

HEN/MRS ALLAN (*alarmed*). 'Tell her to get out of the way, silly – '

IZ/MR ALLAN. '…No, Aunt Allan…'

CATH. 'And the carriage to be borne up into the air and the next thing we know us hurled violently from it.'

HEN/MRS ALLAN (*alarmed*). 'What?!'

CATH. 'A swarm of highwaymen and the old woman now revealed as the highwaywoman-in-chief…'

IZ/MR ALLAN. 'She is describing something from one of those novels she is so fond of.'

CATH. '…no longer in disguise and with pistols in her britches and a glint in her eye.'

HEN/MRS ALLAN. 'Oh, I see, Uncle Allan…'

IZ/MR ALLAN. 'Her pa did warn me she will do this…'

HEN/MRS ALLAN. 'Is it from *The Castle of Otranto*?'

CATH. 'The highwaywoman in britches scooping up the young girl who was travelling in the carriage *quite alone*…'

HEN/MRS ALLAN. 'Or *The Ghost-Seer*, I like that one…'

CATH. 'Her shivering in nothing but her thin white chemise and the highwaywoman in britches making away with her on a big powerful horse.'

HEN/MRS ALLAN. 'Oooh or *The Misfortunes of Virtue*.'

CATH. 'No.

It's not.

(*Surprised*.) Not any of those.

I normally know precisely where my imaginings come from.

How strange.'

HEN/MRS ALLAN *and* IZ/MR ALLAN *exchange indulgent looks.*

HEN. The journey south and into the second act of Catherine's life continued.

IZ. There was no old woman…

HEN. Other than Aunt Allan.

IZ. Or dashingly mysterious highwaywomen scooping up innocent virgins in thin white chemises.

CATH. But it was only extremely dull.

HEN. Especially after Aunt Allan had run out of her supply of comfits, which she did keep secreted about her not-insubstantial person.

IZ. And anecdotes of her own not-very-misspent youth.

HEN/MRS ALLAN (*finishing an anecdote that she alone finds very funny*). '…And I never have since been able to look a codfish in the face without blushing!'

IZ. Owing to a small hole in the canvas, a consistent trickle did start down Cath's back.

HEN. But the weather neither intensified to storming, nor was there any abatement in the dripping.

CATH. Aunt Allan did at one point…

HEN/MRS ALLAN *is riffling through a large carpet bag.*

HEN/MRS ALLAN. '…have a fear that I have left my clogs behind in that last inn…'

IZ/MR ALLAN. 'Oh that would be most inconvenient!'

HEN/MRS ALLAN. 'I only bought them last spring and a very good pair they are too, with a sturdy heel and…'

HEN/MRS ALLAN *stands up, bending over, her bum in the air as they take a corner.* CATH *has to steady her.* IZ/MR ALLAN *has also joined in the search by now.*

CATH. But in the end the fear of this great tragedy did prove to be groundless.

IZ/MR ALLAN. 'Ah-ha! Aunt Allan!'

IZ/MR ALLAN *pulls out a pair of clogs triumphantly. They kiss and tickle companionably, like two very contented older married people.* CATH *is a bit disgusted; the way younger people often are when older people express any sort of affection.*

Scene Two

The muffled thump of music.

CATH. The season had barely begun when I arrived in Bath that spring.

IZ/MRS ALLAN. 'Oh it is too much!'

CATH. And yet the Upper Rooms on Upper Street were already heaving with bright-faced young men and women...

IZ/MRS ALLAN. 'Pushed between people and up against / them.'

HEN. Because Cath has titled this scene...

CATH. Which is Act Two, Scene Two...

IZ *and* HEN.... 'Balls at Last'.

IZ/MRS ALLAN. 'One can barely move! Squeezed closer than one has been to some of one's own family!'

HEN. Mrs Allan proclaimed...

CATH. Because now she is being Aunt Allan in this part, because he has to, you will see that / he has [another role in this scene].

HEN. I've another most important role in this bit.

IZ. But before that.

CATH. Trapped near the entrance we could see nothing of the formal dancing but...

IZ/MRS ALLAN. '...the high feathers of some of the ladies' hats! Oh it is too too vexing!'

CATH....crammed so close that any notions of myself and Mrs Allan taking...

IZ. As Cath had wistfully imagined before she arrived in the town...

CATH (*wistfully*). '...several turns about the room...'

IZ. Were quickly dispelled. (*As* MRS ALLAN.) 'Oh, our Cath, I feel as though I were an egg squashed into the pickle jar, and no nicer smelling some of them are. They might all think themselves very clever and quite the thing indeed, but have their mothers not taught them how to have a wash?'

CATH *shrugs, still excited.*

CATH. Nevertheless it was all *most* exciting because it was the most amount of people I had ever seen in my short life.

HEN. The previous high count being two summers before this at an agricultural show in a neighbouring village and at which Nigel won a prize for his cock.

CATH. But anyway…

IZ. But anyway, it seems that Cath has brought something of the agricultural with her, because loitering by the door, a group of the aforementioned young men espies / our heroine…

IZ/YOUNG GENTLEMAN (*interrupting*). 'A new filly!'

IZ/YOUNG GENTLEMAN 2. 'That narrow little thing.'

IZ/YOUNG GENTLEMAN. 'Not narrow of calf. I spied her legs as she came down from a very dull country carriage, brown horses.'

IZ/YOUNG GENTLEMAN 2. 'My father's estate has farms…'

CATH (*trying to interrupt*). Because / before this…

IZ/YOUNG GENTLEMAN 3. 'We know, farmer boy!'

IZ/YOUNG GENTLEMAN 2. 'He owns land, which he leases to the tenant farmers who work it like the *peasants* that they are! And on one of those farms there is a milkmaid. She has calves like that and thighs too, so useful for walking and bending and squatting. For pushing and / running…

CATH. Because before this I thought I looked rather fine…

IZ/YOUNG GENTLEMAN 2 (*miming suggestively*). '…and riding!'

CATH. In my new dress, with my hair neatly done…

IZ/YOUNG GENTLEMAN 2. 'A real country girl…'

CATH. And I had had a bath only eight days previously, unlike
a lot of my fellow attendees.

IZ/YOUNG GENTLEMAN 3. 'Well versed in cunt-ry matters!
Gfawwww… / hhhawhaawwww…'

IZ/VARIOUS GENTLEMEN *snort and wheeze with the
hilarity of themselves as:*

CATH (*raising her voice to be heard*). But the point is… what
happened next…

HEN. Because Cath intended the first part as an infant to adult,
coming-of-age, or as the Germans would put it…

CATH (*doing the German*). *Bildungsroman.*

HEN. But this next part she means as a romance, so in this
moment the crowds do part,

CATH. And the tall and mysterious and, yes, very handsome
man does emerge…

HEN *emerges. He tries to look as tall and mysterious and so
on, as* CATH *has described.*

And time seems to stop.

Time stops, and the music with it…

Something brooding in his eyes and in his brow…

HEN *adjusts his expression according to* CATH*'s
instruction…*

And he looks to me in all my embarrassment and he looks
around to them and their practically drooling mouths and /
he spits…

HEN. I spit: 'How witty, Charles. And we all know how little
experience you have of such matters!'

CATH *is delighted with* HEN. HEN *is also delighted with
himself.*

IZ/MRS ALLAN *interrupts this moment and time and the music starts again as:*

IZ/MRS ALLAN. 'Master Tilney!'

HEN (*to* IZ/MRS ALLAN). '…Mrs Allan…'

IZ/MRS ALLAN. 'Oh I am so glad you are here.'

HEN. 'Thank you – '

IZ/MRS ALLAN. 'Here and out in society…'

HEN. 'And who might I ask / is this?'

IZ/MRS ALLAN. 'Because when Mr Allan and I heard about your…

Did you get our letter, Hen pet?'

HEN. 'Yes. I…'

IZ/MRS ALLAN. 'One never knows quite what to say in these circumstances, of course, but always better to say *something* I think.'

HEN. 'Well. Yes. I suppose / so.'

IZ/MRS ALLAN. 'And you got the dripping cakes and other perishable stuff?'

HEN. '…That is to say, my sister was most touched by your words.'

IZ/MRS ALLAN. 'Because we did want to visit but I know that your father…

Well, he is a most private man / and…'

HEN. 'Yes…'

IZ/MRS ALLAN. 'Food always cheers me up.

…As you can see!

Oh, but I am going on.'

CATH (*impatiently*). Which she was.

IZ/MRS ALLAN. 'I am just so glad to see you out and about and looking so well!'

CATH. She said again, repeating herself.

IZ. And at this juncture Mrs Allan envelops Mr Tilney into a somewhat bosomy embrace.

HEN *and* IZ/MRS ALLAN *hug*.

HEN *extracts himself*.

HEN. 'I don't think we've met before.'

CATH. 'Oh…'

HEN (*pointedly*). 'And I have not yet had the pleasure of being properly introduced.'

IZ/MRS ALLAN. 'Oh indeed! Cath, this is Henry Tilney, your Uncle Allan's works occupy some of the land that Henry's father, General Tilney, that is, owns.'

HEN. 'They are a kind of business partners.'

IZ/MRS ALLAN. 'After a fashion! Such a sweet boy you are! Master Tilney, may I introduce the apple of mine and Mr Allan's eye, our precious…'

IZ/MRS ALLAN. 'Catherine Morland.'

CATH (*simultaneous*). 'Katerina de Morland.'

IZ/MRS ALLAN (*simultaneous*). 'Cath!'

CATH (*hissingly, to* IZ/MRS ALLAN). 'I had thought to change it!'

HEN. 'What a beautiful name. May I?'

IZ/MRS ALLAN *gives her assent*.

CATH. And so this is the part where I met him. In this moment. The crowds parted like that and he said those things with a kind of brooding. Something brooding in his eyes and in his brow like I said. And so I, your most romantical of heroines, as you would expect, am quite ready to be swept away and also off my feet…

Scene Three

Dancing with a Boy

HEN *and* CATH *dance*.

HEN *and* CATH *slow*.

HEN. '…your aunt…'

CATH. 'Yes. I have known her since I was little.'

HEN. 'That is so often the way with aunts.'

> *They dance*.
>
> *They slow*.
>
> 'Coal.'

CATH. 'Sorry?'

HEN. 'Her husband, that is to say your Uncle Allan, who is, as your aunt said, a friend of my father's, who you will also have known no doubt since your inception… he is in mines – '

CATH. 'Yes. I think so. Something like that…why?' (*Looking a bit bored*.) 'Is your father also… in… mines?'

HEN. 'No. Oh no. He doesn't have an… occupation.'

CATH. 'I see.'

HEN. 'Not that I think there would be anything wrong with… that.'

CATH. 'No. Well, why would you?'

HEN. 'Of course not. But we are simply, that is to say that we are not "in" anything. As a family.'

CATH. 'Pa is in… Jesus. Or Jesus is in him. That is to say – a vicar.'

> *They dance*.
>
> *They slow*.

HEN. And Catherine found herself sighing at this point in our frustratingly slow perambulation about the crowded floor.

CATH. Only a little.

HEN *indicates encouragingly that she should do the sigh*.

CATH *sighs*.

They dance.

They slow.

HEN (*with the air of throwing in the towel*). 'I shall make but a poor figure in your journal tonight.'

CATH. 'My journal?'

HEN. 'Yes, I know exactly what you will write: "Friday, went to the Upper Rooms, wore my best sprigged-muslin robe with pale-blue trimmings – plain black – "'

CATH. Not that plain. They had new ribbons and I had shined them.

HEN. 'Plain black shoes – appeared to much advantage; but was harassed by a pack of half-witted men who had no business being in polite society and then was made to dance with a strange fellow who distressed me with his / nonsense…'

CATH. 'You understand muslins, sir?'

HEN. 'I am allowed to be an excellent judge.'

CATH (*encouragingly*). 'And you said before that you liked mine…'

HEN. 'It is very pretty, madam, but I do not think it will wash well…'

CATH. 'Wash well?'

HEN. 'I am afraid that it will fray. As I say, I am allowed to be an excellent judge myself and my sister has often trusted me in the choice of gown. I bought one for her the other day, and it was pronounced to be a prodigious bargain by all who saw it. I gave but five shillings a yard for it and a true Indian muslin…'

CATH. 'It is… unusual, is it not, for a sister to entrust her brother with that most feminine of tasks.'

HEN. 'I do not think so. If circumstances dictate it.'

Beat.

They dance.

(*Unable to stop himself.*) 'Why should I not buy the materials for a dress?'

They slow.

'Why should I not have it made up in the most flattering and wearable of modern designs and returned to her post haste by carriage. And her sending by return a note to say how delighted in it she was. And that wearing it after the most terrible months we have recently had to endure and only about our cold and draughty abbey where there is no reason for its wearing whatsoever apart from for her own satisfaction, has lifted her spirits immeasurably. Just as I intended.

I do not see that there is anything wrong with that. And to say there is strikes me as exceedingly ignorant!'

CATH (*excited*). 'You said...'

HEN. 'What?'

CATH. 'Just now, you said your sister...'

HEN. 'Ellie. Keeper of all my secrets, my best friend and the recipient of the most flattering and wearable dresses in the / whole county of...'

CATH. 'Yes. Her. You said that she wore that peculiar brother-bought dress, although she had no occasion for it... (*Trying not to get too excited.*) That she wore it whilst about an... An abbey.'

HEN. 'Why yes. I am sorry. I assumed your aunt had told you. I am Henry Tilney, son of General Tilney of Northanger Abbey.'

CATH. 'You are then... your family are an... an abbey...'

HEN. 'Yes. *It is*. Indeed. Our home is a very ancient and enormous and actually pretty inconveniently grand family seat not fifty miles east of here.'

CATH (*breathlessly*). 'And have you got battlements?!'

HEN. '*It* does. Yes. Why?'

CATH. 'Well…'

> CATH *is so beside herself that she cannot actually speak.*

HEN. 'Shall I tell you what I think you ought to write in your journal about me?'

CATH. 'Oh… um…'

HEN. 'I danced with a young man; had a great deal of conversation with him…'

CATH. 'Oh right…'

HEN. ' – seems an extraordinary genius – '

CATH. 'I see…'

HEN. 'Especially on the subject of muslins. I hope I may come to know more of him.'

CATH (*attempting to sound playful*). 'Ah! But, after all, perhaps, I keep no journal, Mr Tilney.'

> *They dance.*

> *They slow.*

IZ. And it was at this juncture, when both parties seemed to have no obvious conversational route forward, that Henry Tilney decided to more fully deploy the instructions of a pamphlet that he had recently been commended to consult by that same parental figure already mentioned.

HEN. 'Not keep a journal!'

IZ. What this pamphlet instructed in was the art of communication with the fairer sex…

HEN. 'How are the memories of various dresses to be gathered, and the particular state of your complexion, and curl of your hair to be described in all their diversities, without constant recourse to a journal?'

IZ. Specifically the art of communication with the fairer sex for those lacking natural aptitude or experience or… interest in those delicate matters.

HEN. 'Then once you have gathered, altered to show you in the best possible light, and recorded meticulously so that on some future date your young female relatives might have the pleasure of living these event vicariously through you, detailing all the fascinating events they missed, still residing as they no doubt do in the small and narrow place that you come from.'

IZ. The pamphlet had only one key suggestion: that the seducing gentleman should find some small faults in the woman who he was hoping to affect or seduce…

HEN. 'Which is probably somewhere in the north.'

IZ. And that once he has found these faults that he should proceed to tease her on these matters.

HEN (*panickingly, he really can't seem to stop*). The problem with such an instruction being that once one has started down this path it is quite impossible to stop, even when one senses it is not producing the desired effect: 'Ha ha ha.'

CATH *looks quite annoyed, but keeps dancing determinedly with* HEN.

'Because as far as I have had the opportunity of judging, it appears to me that the usual style of writing among women is faultless, except three particulars.'

CATH (*trying to be playful*). 'And what, pray, are they?'

HEN. '…a total inattention to logography.'

IZ. (Spellings.)

CATH. 'Upon my word!'

HEN. 'A very frequent ignorance of punctuation.'

CATH. 'Good heavens…'

HEN. 'And most egregious of all, a general deficiency of any interesting subject matter at all…'

CATH. 'Upon my word but you are a rude young man.'

HEN. 'You are a very disagreeable young woman!'

CATH. 'I believe that you are being contrary on purpose, in order to provoke me!'

HEN. 'I believe that you do not even understand that you are being contradictory!'

CATH. 'Oh you are infuriating!'

HEN. 'Not as infuriating as you!'

They break apart from dancing, abruptly.

Scene Four

CATH *is disagreeing with* HEN *about the last scene. They are trying not to be overheard by the audience.*

HEN. We had.

CATH. Yes, I know –

HEN. Crossed words. That is what / what happened so…

CATH. But it… I do not disagree but I say that the *tenor* of those disagreements… Because the way we just did it, just now, was not passionate… romantic… it was. We descended into…

HEN. We bickered a little.

CATH. Exactly.

HEN. And it is true I did think you a bit of an affected and / inconsistent…

CATH. Oh!

HEN. But not *just* affected and inconsistent, other things too…

CATH. What other things?

HEN. Well.

Beat.

You were funny.

CATH. Funny?

HEN. Yes…

CATH. Romantic heroines are not meant to be funny.

HEN.… Aren't they? Oh. And you were fun. You were very playful and that / was –

CATH. Oh! I am to be given all the qualities of a much-loved family pet!

HEN. And you did not simply. I liked that you told me when you disagreed with me. I had never met a young woman who did that. At least. It reminded me. Well, it reminded me of my sister / which…

CATH. Oh. Your sister! Is that any better than a dog? Romantic heroines are not meant to remind people of their sisters. I will not repeat again what I found you.

CATH *becomes aware that the audience can hear them arguing.*

(*To* HEN.) Fine then. (*To* IZ.) Let's just get on with it.

Scene Five

The Morning After the Night Before

CATH. Henry Tilney had indicated as he left the Upper Rooms that night that he would be away from Bath for the following few days.

HEN *mistakenly assumes he will be playing himself in this part:*

HEN (*simultaneous*). 'I must… go away. On a matter most.'

IZ/HEN (*simultaneous*). 'I must… go away. On a matter most.'

HEN. 'It is to do with my family and those matters which…'

CATH *and* IZ *stare at* HEN – *he will not be required to play himself in this part.*

He reluctantly leaves.

IZ/HEN. 'I am prevented from saying precisely what on account of it not being quite appropriate for me to divulge such delicate family matters…'

CATH/HEN. '…matters that I will insist on making quite heavy and suggestive weather of all evening…'

IZ/HEN. '…but which I will not reveal directly to you, a simple northern lass from the countryside…'

CATH/HEN. '…who could not possibly…'

IZ/HEN. 'Because of you being so very simple…'

CATH/HEN. '…and northern…'

IZ/HEN. 'and also on account of the rather large stick up / my [bum].'

CATH. He did hint that he might like to see me on his return. And your heroine did find that this absence threw a fresh grace in her imagination around his person and manners and increased her society to know more of him. Whether she prepared herself to bed to dream of him that night…

IZ. Or whether she fell into her normal dreamless stupor...

CATH....We cannot say. This being a very proper sort of story we do not have access to her bedchamber. The next day your heroine, that is to say I... I was encouraged by my aunt that I should not sit in waiting while my suitor was engaged elsewhere.

IZ. And who only said he *might* see her on his return.

CATH. But that instead the right and proper thing to do would be to venture out. Patting my leg in the way that she liked to do and offering me one of her now-replenished supply of confectionary and encouraging me to the company of my own sex.

HEN/MRS ALLAN. 'Because, flower, as your mam always says to me, friendship is certainly the finest balm for the pangs of any sort of... disappointed love.'

Scene Six

Making a Friend

IZ. 'Hello.'

CATH. 'Hello.'

IZ. 'Dull, isn't it.'

CATH. 'What?'

IZ. 'This.'

CATH. Because the next day...

IZ. 'All this.'

CATH....the next afternoon I find myself in the Pump Room.

IZ. 'Standing around in cold rooms waiting to be noticed...'

CATH. And there are not so many younger people today. Indeed it seems to be in the majority those who have come to Bath for their various ailments. A proliferation of matriarchs in wheeled chairs.

IZ. Most aptly called bath chairs.

CATH. And gouty men on sticks. And Aunt and Uncle Allan are in their element, of course. Talking animatedly with some distant relatives about their various medical complaints, the way that older people do like to do with other older people.

IZ. As if they were fascinating. And this is when you get talking to the only other young lady in the room. 'You were at that dance last night. In the Upper Rooms.'

CATH. 'Yes, I...'

IZ. 'You were having trouble with those awful men.'

CATH. 'Oh. You saw that...'

IZ. 'I noticed you.'

CATH. 'I see. But. I expect they were just being... mischievous.'

IZ. 'Look at that man's leg sores!'

CATH. 'They say it is because of port and other rich stuff.'

IZ. 'I hope not, as I intend to feast on all that sort of thing when I am older and married to a rich man.'

CATH. 'How exciting! But how do you know he will be definitely rich?'

IZ. And so this is where I enter your story.

CATH. And where she and I, my new acquaintance, discuss our prospects. And I describe the most disagreeable but also broodingly mysterious man that I have met the evening before. And I ask her if she saw him last night too?

IZ. But I say I did not.

CATH. And I do ask her what young man she...

IZ *smirks at* CATH *and raises her eyebrow.*

But before I can finish my question she has already raised a brow and confesses to a most utilitarian approach to what she calls the marriage problem.

IZ. 'I do have a minimum figure in my head which is the income that he must earn, or better receive, in order that I would seriously consider a proposal.'

CATH. 'Oh!'

IZ. 'I would also like someone who doesn't make me feel sick to my stomach just looking at him.'

CATH. 'How queer you are!'

IZ. She exclaims. And I reply.

'Yes. I am. Very.'

And so it is at this point that Miss Isabella Thorpe.

CATH. For that is her very handsome name.

IZ. Suggests…

CATH. She persuades me that our growing attachment cannot be satisfied with whispered words exchanged in a Pump Room…

IZ. …filled with the depressingly old and infirm hoping to stave off the Grim Reaper for a few more underwhelming years…

CATH. But instead requires that we should quit it altogether. 'But what about our chaperones, my aunt… and you must have…'

IZ. 'I do not have anyone – '

CATH. 'Oh!'

IZ. 'Nor do I need anyone, Cath!'

CATH. And despite my protestations this girl pulls me quite away.

IZ. 'I am quite capable of minding myself!'

CATH. Through a door.

IZ. Cut into the very wall which Cath had not even noticed…

CATH. Until this moment!

IZ. And onto…

Scene Seven

A Hero

Like magic they are on:

CATH.…a street.

IZ. On a curve. Grand white houses.

CATH. A crescent of a moon of modern wedding cakes. And all the people…

IZ. Like the figurines atop those cakes…

CATH. But not trapped in icing…

IZ. Instead drifting…

CATH. Drifting in pairs and threes in such a manner as suggests they have no feet at all!

IZ. And hardly any. Hardly any people at all 'because it has no business calling itself a city…'

CATH. 'This is the biggest…'

IZ. '…when it is barely a town, barely a place…'

CATH. '…it's the biggest and busiest place I have ever been!'

IZ. 'Because where I am from, this country's proper capital, my home is, it is close to the river, the boats all jostling for room and the houses tumbling higgledy-piggledy down to the water…'

CATH. 'Oh!'

IZ. '…and the people, such a diversity of people, that a person who does not want to be noticed, if they are clever they can dress in such a way that they do not draw attention. If a gentleman's greatcoat and waistcoat are only of a simple colour and she has pulled her cap low she might not be perceived at all…'

CATH. 'You didn't!'

IZ. 'Don't I?'

CATH. 'You couldn't.

I think you are teasing me.'

I say. But in this moment I know that she is not. Because I can see her now. Her greatcoat and waistcoat.

IZ. And she does picture Isabella like this, turning in a busy urban street quite unnoticed and winking back.

A moment between them.

But then:

CATH. 'I would not like to go to London anyway, or not that London that you are describing, I should not like to be in amongst all that chaos of strange people, I would not like the smells and the noise or the dirt.'

IZ. 'But you like it here? Where it is impossible not to be noticed.'

CATH. 'Why would you not want to be noticed? What would be the purpose of that?' But she only shrugs. Smiles again in that way of hers. And I do feel so flattered that she confides all this in me as we round corners and stroll along broad boulevards.

IZ. Even the sun is clean and pale as it sinks down.

CATH. And the clocks strike the hour over and over, as I talk and walk with her. She, my new friend…

IZ. And they are, they have been walking in curves, chattering in circles and they both know it is getting far too late but they do not say anything, either of them.

CATH. As we reveal ourselves to each other.

IZ. When suddenly, in front of them.

CATH. And in red. All in red.

IZ. The young gentleman from the Upper Rooms the previous night. (*Folding her arms.*) And their arms folding.

CATH. And they smell, they have a smell…

IZ. They have been drinking beer in an alehouse all day.

CATH. And one of them takes a step forward.

IZ *steps forward.*

And he smiles…

IZ/YOUNG GENTLEMAN 2. 'Oh it is with the farmer girl.'

CATH.…only the smile does not quite reach his eyes…

IZ/YOUNG GENTLEMAN 2. 'The one with calves like that and her suggestive ankles…'

CATH. Because he is one of the pack of men who embarrassed our heroine the night before.

IZ. But he was also the man who was harassing Isabella Thorpe for many nights before that in the street and at the Pump Room and around the Upper Rooms because these kind of men do stalk the kind of person Isabella is, just for the sport of it…

CATH. And he is moving towards us now, sniffing, and all their mouths, the whole pack salivating with anticipation of us as he snarls…

IZ/YOUNG GENTLEMAN 2. '…because you should be careful being out without a chaperone this late, even if you are from a city, because you are right, this is a town not a city, and it belongs to men like us…'

CATH/YOUNG GENTLEMAN 3. '…and with those lips and those hips of yours, *girl*, which are made for men like us to take just / as we please…'

IZ. But before it is fully out of his mouth…

CATH *throws a punch.*

CATH/YOUNG GENTLEMAN 3 *has been punched; his chin jolts up.*

The blow, soft and hard, catches him on the bottom of his jaw and he is sent off balance.

CATH/YOUNG GENTLEMAN 3 *staggers backwards.*

CATH. He is staggering backwards and all these lads…

IZ. …this crescent of soldiers.

CATH. Staring down at him, their friend who has just been hit by a girl.

CATH/YOUNG GENTLEMAN 3*'s nose is bleeding. She wipes her nose and looks down at the blood on her hand, surprised.*

And my fist is shaking. My heart is beating in my chest. And in this moment I feel. Looking down at him and up at her face…

IZ. And this is when Isabella shouts to Cath to 'Run!'

Scene Eight

IZ and CATH are still a bit overexcited and giggly from the last scene.

CATH. And during the fourteen days that followed, Isabella and Catherine went ribbon shopping and to dances and for many more walks about the town, just as new friends are apt to do.

IZ. And if a rainy-day afternoon deprived them of other enjoyments, they were resolute in defiance of wet and dirt and shut themselves up to read those now quite well-worn novels together.

CATH. (Each more dreadful than the last.) And so there can be no doubt that the friendship between these two has been established. And now it is two weeks later. And today, and in this part, we find Isabella and Catherine in the back of a two-horse open carriage.

IZ. But first, because in order for what follows to make sense we must do the agreement. The agreement between these two. So some time between those two events on one of those rainy afternoons...

CATH. Wrapped up in the same blanket and quite content.

IZ. Your warm head laid in my lap and our fingers interlaced. You ventured...

CATH. 'My older brother is visiting Bath next week.

Sensible James who I have not mentioned to this point who is older and... sensible and visiting the town on a brief holiday from his sensible degree at his sensible university.

And who knows your own brother a little.

Such a strange coincidence.'

Do IZ and CATH look round at the audience: this really is a very helpful 'coincidence'...

IZ (*still reading*). 'Mmmm.'

CATH. 'You know.

I had a fancy.

Now you must not say I am being silly.'

IZ (*teasingly*). 'Oh, you are never silly, Cath.'

CATH. 'But I have a fancy that if each brother were to meet the other's sister.

Perhaps if we were to arrange some… excursion.

Because if we were to marry each other's brothers…

Because then we would be each other's sisters.'

IZ. 'Sisters?!'

CATH. 'In-law I mean. Because we are now' …as we have established… 'such close female friends, indeed you are quite the closest I have ever had.'

IZ. 'And if we were sisters-in-law it would be quite proper that we should visit each other as frequently as we would wish. Well that is… Cath… that would be…'

I say.

Because this is when the agreement was made.

CATH. When we discussed an arrangement. 'Oh, but it is only a fancy!' I did say. 'Born of my quite ridiculous imagination!'

Scene Nine

Two Weeks Later

CATH *and* IZ *are sitting high up, in the back of a two-horse open carriage which is not moving. It is raining.*

CATH. And so now it is definitely two weeks later. And we find Isabella and Catherine in the back of a two-horse open carriage.

IZ. About to go out on the excursion agreed in the last scene, with our brothers...

CATH. That is Isabella's brother, John Thorpe.

HEN/JOHN THORPE *appears, he stands near where the head of the horse would be...*

HEN/JOHN THORPE. 'What-ho, ladies!'

CATH. And my brother, Sensible James...

They both are unsure what to do about representing JAMES.

...Who we do not have need of physically representing as he is not very memorable and does not play a very important part in this story. And as Isabella and Catherine are sat up here discussing that outing, the men are stood down there talking about the sort of thing men like to talk about...

HEN/JOHN THORPE *is momentarily unsure what to say.*

HEN/JOHN THORPE (*trying his best with the horse bantz*). '...Ahhh... but only look at his hooves... notice his... flanks...'

IZ. And this is when she says it...

HEN/JOHN THORPE. 'Behold his... LOINS...'

CATH. 'Because,' I say, 'I know we have an arrangement to go to this castle you mention – '

IZ. Which is called Blaise Castle and which Cath had said she especially wanted to visit.

CATH. 'Because I do. I do have every desire to ride out with our two brothers, just as we had arranged...'

IZ....But.

CATH. 'But.' Because our heroine has heard word that Henry Tilney is back in Bath today and she knows he may come to call for her. 'And if we are to make this... quite fanciful excursion then after all I will not be in when he calls. And then it will be most rude.'

IZ. 'Yes, I understand.'

CATH. 'So you see my predicament.'

IZ. 'Of course.

But he did only say he might call, did he not?

And you did promise you would ride out with us. That is what we agreed, Cath.'

Beat.

'Very well, then there is an end to the party. (*Shouting down to* HEN/JOHN THORPE.) We are not going.'

HEN/JOHN THORPE. 'Whattttt?!'

IZ. 'I say we cannot go! Cath says she will not ride out with us to the castle. And if Cath does not ride, I cannot. Having no chaperone or companion I cannot be the only female. So we shall all have to stay in waiting for this Tilney fellow to call for her, who probably won't...'

HEN/JOHN THORPE. 'Ah... tish-poo, bother and damnation!'

IZ. '...and what a miserable day indeed!'

HEN/JOHN THORPE. 'Indeed!'

It rains harder.

CATH. And she looks. In this moment she is looking out at the rain and her jaw has set the way I have seen it do before when she is angry about something.

And so. Even though the proper thing to do in this moment would have been for your romantic heroine to stay in and wait for Henry Tilney of Northanger Abbey to call I cannot help but: 'Is it a very fine sort of castle?'

IZ. 'You told me it is the finest place in England.'

CATH. 'And is it very very old?'

IZ. 'The oldest, they say.'

CATH. 'But is it like what one reads about?'

IZ. 'Exactly. The very same. With all the requisites one would expect of a most haunted and romantical ruined building!'

CATH. 'OOOOOOOHHHHHH! Let's go to Blaise Castle and have a terrible adventure.'

IZ and CATH are tickling each other and giggling…

HEN/JOHN THORPE. 'AHEM.'

They remember HEN/JOHN THORPE. *They break apart.*

'I insist you must come with me, Miss Morland. And Izzy can follow with your brother in his little horse-and-cart arrangement. Each of us shall take the other's sister!'

HEN/JOHN THORPE *mounts the carriage with enthusiasm.*

'Huzzah!'

Scene Ten

Little Horse-and-Cart Arrangement

CATH *and* HEN/JOHN THORPE *are in the carriage, going at a good-ish speed.*

They are forced to slow.

HEN/JOHN THORPE. 'Pshhhh!'

CATH. 'Oh…'

HEN/JOHN THORPE. 'Bother and damnation again, Catherine Morland! Your brother is pulling out ahead of me.'

CATH. 'Ah, yes, I can see that.'

HEN/JOHN THORPE. 'I have been forced to slow.'

CATH. 'I know, John Thorpe.'

HEN/JOHN THORPE. 'I had intended that we should lead…'

CATH. 'I can see that quite well with my own eyes. But I am sure he did not mean to annoy you. It is just this traffic, it makes it quite impossible to…'

HEN/JOHN THORPE. '…and do behold the behind of his overtaking carriage, because there is not a sound piece of iron about it. I have never seen such a quivering backside in my life. His wheels have been fairly worn out and as for the body! It is the most devilish little rickety business that I ever beheld! Thank God you are in a better one with me, eh?'

Beat, a moment of inspiration for CATH.

CATH. 'Do you think your sister will be all right riding in it with my brother? As you say, it is a very rickety business altogether and indeed, and it is likely to be quite a bumpy drive once we are out of Bath. Perhaps we should swap.'

HEN/JOHN THORPE. 'Oh…'

CATH. Says John Thorpe, a man who does himself resemble a large horse.

HEN. With muscled calves and trimmed waist.

CATH. 'Or better still she should ride with us both.'

HEN. The kind of man who looks like he himself could be ready to pull a large cart at the drop of a pretty lady's bonnet.

CATH. 'I think there is room for three.'

HEN/JOHN THORPE. 'I would not worry.'

CATH. 'Or maybe we should not be going out on a day such as this at all, after all.'

HEN/JOHN THORPE. 'My sister intended to be quite distracted, oh yes indeed, quite distracted by the company on this long journey out into the country.'

CATH (*worried*). 'Oh. Is it so very far?

HEN/JOHN THORPE. 'It is quite far enough for her business I can assure you, ha ha…'

They turn a corner.

CATH. And we have just turned into one of the grandest crescents in Bath, where the Tilneys have their house. And as we slow I see the door of the Tilney house slowly open and I see Henry Tilney and a most comely woman stepping out. His hand about her waist in a most familiar manner and he has said something that has made her laugh as they step down onto the pavement… and I… my heart is… I feel completely…

And as we near I see Henry and he sees me and he waves (*Waving, she waves through the following*.) and I wave in return. 'Oh! John Thorpe, it is Henry Tilney, we should stop as I did say that I would go for a walk with him on his return…'

HEN. But it seems to Cath that John Thorpe has not heard her, as he cracks the whip on the back of his horse to 'Giddy-up!'

The carriage jolts forward and CATH *is forced to stop waving.*

And pulls out, dodging around Cath's brother's horse and cart…

(*As* JOHN THORPE.) 'RARRRR!'

CATH. 'Oh, are we not going too / fast…'

HEN/JOHN THORPE. 'I assure you we are not going anywhere near as fast as we might be.'

CATH. 'And because Mr Henry Tilney will think me very rude indeed for speeding off like this and it is not, I do not think it is [safe] – '

HEN/JOHN THORPE. 'I have been almost twice as fast in this – '

CATH *is trying to look back at where they came from. She gives up. Turns around again. They are going very fast now.*

'Your brother is a fool.'

CATH (*still distracted*). 'What?'

HEN/JOHN THORPE. 'We have left him and my sister quite behind ha ha ha. I have told him he is foolish for not getting a better horse and gig.'

CATH. 'No, he is not, for I am sure he cannot afford it.'

HEN/JOHN THORPE. 'And why cannot he afford it?'

CATH. 'Because he has not money enough.'

HEN/JOHN THORPE. 'And whose fault is that?'

CATH. 'Nobody's, that I know of. That is to say. He is only a student and our family is quite frugal.'

HEN/JOHN THORPE. 'Frugal. Ha!' But at this point Cath is so distracted by the speed they are going at and the possibility of who that mysterious lady was who Henry Tilney / was with…

CATH.…had his arm wrapped round in a most intimate manner…

HEN. That she does not hear what John Thorpe says next as they speed faster and faster: (*As* JOHN THORPE.) 'I expect that Izzy has told you our father is of the professional classes. So that is why Izzy does not have very nice things and why she must make do without a chaperone and with only her older brother for protection who is, as you will have gathered, of quite raffish reputation. Ha ha. But our mother is from a good family and I have told them both I do not intend to take up any sort of occupation at all. So to speak frankly, you need not worry. Being the oldest son I expect to come into a not-insufficient fortune from my mother's side. It is simply a matter of finding a wife and settling down and putting aside my errant ways and then I have been assured that there is a decent trust fund...'

CATH. 'Oh?'

HEN/JOHN THORPE. 'Oh yes! Are you and your brother going to the mid-season ball next Tuesday?'

CATH. 'Oh yes, that is I am not sure, it depends on – '

HEN/JOHN THORPE. 'Good, then we shall all four go together.'

CATH. 'Oh well...'

HEN/JOHN THORPE. 'I will countenance no objections, Catherine Morland. Some people can be rather snobbish, but you will find no such silliness in my Izzy (being a girl and so without an inherited fortune like mine she cannot afford to be picky!), and as for myself, well, as I say being the first-born son I have good fortune from my mother's side which is old money so I am very much free to choose as I please... giddy-up, giddy-up...'

CATH. And John Thorpe does at this moment encourage the horses on even more, cracking the whip...

HEN/JOHN THORPE. 'Rarrrrr!'

CATH. And I grip the seat as I venture: 'John Thorpe, I really think that we ought to slow...'

HEN/JOHN THORPE. 'Oh nonsense, Catherine Morland, what are you afraid of?'

CATH. And as we speed faster and faster I cannot stop thinking of Henry Tilney of Northanger Abbey staring after me wondering at why it is I did not stop for him. But the next thing I remember is...

The sound of the beginning of a crash.

IZ. But for you to understand how *I* feel as I watch my brother's stupid showy shay beginning to tip further and further to one side, as one wheel lifts up into the air and the great scraping grinding noise, which is the sound of the wheel bolt and the wheel loosing away, we have to go back to that night which was two weeks before this, after the bit in the street with the soldiers and Cath's heroics but before the agreement and all that followed…

The sound of the crash stops abruptly.

The noise reverses. It is unsettling.

Scene Eleven

Goodnight / Crash

CATH *and* IZ *are out of breath.*

IZ. We run and we run until our feet ache.

CATH. And our hearts beat in our chests.

IZ. The cries of the man that she has punched and his mates still echoing behind us.

CATH. As she pulls me inside a dark doorway…

IZ. Giggling.

CATH. I watch a trickle of sweat as it runs down her cheek, past her ear and round into the curve of her neck.

IZ. And still, breathless, she confides she reads in order…

CATH. '…to have adventures, adventures like these!'

IZ. And I say, the words all tumbling out at once…

CATH. Isabella says. She says that she reads in order to find herself. But that she has not yet.

IZ. '…on any of the pages of the books that I have read…'

CATH. Sometimes she has seen what she thinks is the back of her own head, but then the character turns...

IZ. 'And it is never me. And do you know how I feel?'

CATH. And I can tell that she wants me to say that I do. That I did understand what that was like, to feel that.

IZ. But I also know that she does not.

CATH. Because I have imagined myself into being any number of duchesses or princesses and I have always, always been able to do that.

IZ. Because girls like her are meant to, aren't they, imagine themselves into all those stories.

CATH. But in this moment, as I feel her heart now, beating inside my chest.

IZ. And those stories are written for girls like her.

CATH. Pressed up against her.

IZ. Not people like me.

CATH. Because I have never met anyone like her and so I cannot imagine what is about to happen between us.

IZ. We do not exist after all. Especially not in any romances. And because perhaps before this moment I have been content to play the role of Miss Isabella Thorpe, your romantic heroine's sharp-tongued best friend.

CATH. Because I have never read a story like this.

IZ. But after this. I become Izzy. Your Iz.

They are very close together now...

Simultaneously:

They kiss.

The sound of a carriage and horses crashing.

Interval.

ACT THREE

Scene One

The Right Path

CATH *starts before the lighting has had a chance to change.*

CATH. So.

Because we have got a bit. Off track. Off the path. But do
not worry because now I will get us back onto it so that it
can lead us to the turreted title of this story and the inevitably
romantical and gothical third act that we have all gathered
here for.

*She indicates to the stage management to change the
lighting.*

(*Officially, she prepared this bit.*) A week ago I was in a
terrible accident. I was riding in a carriage when we were
suddenly borne up, a vast black bird thrust into flight, only to
be dashed in the next moment upon the cold, hard,
unforgiving ground. In that selfsame moment my dearest
friend, Miss Isabella Thorpe, came bowling round the corner
in another carriage, in quick pursuit. Isabella took me up in
her arms. Crying and weeping over my now, it seemed,
almost-dead body. I was, however, soon revived, her tears of
friendship falling warmly onto my cheeks.

HEN *enters, a bit confused by the fact* CATH *has started
without him and* IZ.

Before all that I had also already danced with a tall,
broodingly handsome man. We danced and had most
romantical conversations which turned to quick passionful
rages, as is so often the case with those that are on the edge
of falling into love. He and his *sister*, who I had previously
seen stepping out together and so gained quite the wrong

impression about, not knowing their familial link, dropped a note round at our lodgings a couple of days after the aforementioned terrible tragedy of my near-death experience:

CATH *indicates that* HEN *should perform the note*.

HEN. 'I was... ahem... sorry to hear of your accident...'

CATH....it read...

HEN. '...your aunt and uncle... mentioned... to my father... that you should be recovered enough to attend the forthcoming mid-season ball the day after next. I do hope that I will see you there.

CATH *prompts*...

Kind regards.

Et cetera, et cetera...'

CATH *dismisses* HEN.

HEN *exits*.

CATH. Well, what do you think of that? I have made my most bosom best friend for life and also met probably the love of my life in almost the exact selfsame moment. Henry Tilney of Northanger Abbey has sent me a note that certainly indicates the depths of his great affections towards me, despite his unforthcoming masculine nature. After my terrible accident and resulting not-insubstantial injuries which have led me to have to lie on my fainting couch for over a week, I am now quite recovered and the ball is tonight! Isn't life exciting. Well, maybe not for you all, who are just normal people come here to live vicariously through me but you will see.

IZ *enters, she is holding costumes for the ball*.

IZ. What. What is / this – ?

CATH. Oh, I think I hear Isabella. We are getting ready for the ball together...

Scene Two

Country Dancing

Hubbub. IZ *and* CATH *are standing quite near each other on the women's side.* HEN *is further away on the men's side.*

IZ. 'I am so glad you are recovered, Catherine Morland, and I do not think that your having been indisposed and so unavailable has done your reputation any harm. Indeed on the contrary your suitors, or suitor... such as he is... only seems to grow more ardent in his desire for you.'

CATH. 'Yes...'

The musicians warm up.

IZ. 'Now that the formal part of the evening is over, the real country dancing can commence and we can secure our prospects.'

CATH. 'My brother, Sensible James, has been smiling at you all evening and I think that my... prospect... such as he is...'

IZ. 'Oh he cannot stop looking. I know that you find him a little disagreeable sometimes.'

CATH. 'Indeed...'

IZ. 'But he is so much better than the other suitors who have shown an interest in you. Indeed, one might say he is almost agreeable.'

CATH. 'Indeed, almost. Isabella, I must tell you... this suitor, the suitors we are each discussing in this moment, they are not... [the same person].'

The music starts.

IZ. 'Oh! We must begin!'

They all start a dance.

After a few moments HEN *and* CATH *are thrown together.*

CATH. 'Henry Tilney!'

HEN. 'Oh it is my little novel reader!'

CATH. 'You do not know that I read novels.'

HEN. 'Of course you keep a journal. Of course you read novels. Everything about you demonstrates as much.'

CATH. 'And what is so very wrong with that?'

HEN. 'Well. Nothing, / except…'

CATH. 'I expect when you grow up you will learn how to speak to women.'

HEN. 'Oh, Catherine, you are too teasing!'

CATH. But in this moment and before I can respond to Henry Tilney's playful counter-riposte, we shift. His line dances up the room and mine down and I find myself adjacent to Isabella once again…

HEN and CATH *are obliged to dance away from each other.*

IZ and CATH *are obliged to dance towards each other.*

IZ. 'I think your brother, Sensible James, is quite ensnared. As far as one can tell in a man that does not believe in the use of facial expressions. And now all you have to do is secure your own prospects…'

CATH. 'Yes, but, Isabella.' Because I did try to tell you in this part and before we proceeded further / that…

HEN swaps roles and dances towards CATH *as JOHN THORPE.*

IZ. 'Oh, here he comes, Cath.'

HEN/JOHN THORPE gives a little wave of greeting to CATH, *who is obliged to return it. She does so unenthusiastically…*

(*Having to raise her voice to be heard.*) 'Remember what we agreed…'

CATH is a little drunker than in the previous exchange.

HEN/JOHN THORPE (*mock annoyed*). 'Well... This is a cursed shabby trick to play on John Thorpe! All through the formal dancing you seemed to duck constantly away from me.'

CATH. 'I never promised to dance with you, John Thorpe.'

HEN/JOHN THORPE. 'Pretending to be more interested in that Tilney fellow. Ah but my sister has told me this is all part of "The Game". These ladies' tricks!'

CATH. '...Can we slow for a moment...'

HEN/JOHN THORPE. 'You must always insist on asking John Thorpe to slow! But we must not, it will disturb the whole pattern of dancers, and in any case I only came for the sake of dancing with you and I firmly think you were engaged to me ever since last Monday before we had our crash when you said – '

CATH. 'Please, John, I cannot find my feet and my head feels – '

HEN/JOHN THORPE. 'Still, never mind, we are here now. Despite your games! Or perhaps because of them! Dancing together!'

CATH (*pulling herself together*). 'I am not dancing with anyone, I am dancing near many people, that is the custom for country dancing, is it not? To dance in squares, to tarry in circles and to strip the willow up and down. To tie oneself to one partner exclusively is, as I understand it, terrible bad manners. Our dancing is polymorphous.'

HEN/JOHN THORPE. 'Polymorphous! Polyamorous! Poo, poo! I consider the country dance as an emblem of marriage. Fidelity to one man and complaisance to him are the principal duties of both...'

CATH. '...You know, I think I shall have more wine after this...'

HEN/JOHN THORPE. '...even if you object to being agreeable to a man, to put it another way, you must acknowledge in marriage, the man is supposed to provide for the support of the woman...'

CATH. '…I do not feel in quite the right frame of mind for this bit…'

HEN/JOHN THORPE. '…the woman to make the home agreeable to the man…'

CATH (*pulling herself together again*). 'But in dancing their duties are exactly exchanged; the agreeableness, the compliance, are expected from him. He is to ask, but she is to decide. He might lead but she is the one to choose to follow or not, and in this moment I ask for your compliance, please do not insist that I am dancing with you when I have said that I am not.'

HEN/JOHN THORPE. 'Oh I see, it is like that. You are going to continue with this pretence of preferring him – '

CATH. 'Smile and be agreeable to the fact that I am dancing with everyone, as is the custom…'

The music changes and HEN/JOHN THORPE *and* CATH *are obliged to dance away from each other,* IZ *and* CATH *to dance towards each other.*

IZ. 'Oh look, Tiresome Tilney is making his way down the line yet again.'

CATH. 'Yes I know he. But I, maybe I do not find him [tiresome].' We are about to dance with each other once again in this part, and before that: 'Because I must tell you that our arrangement…' Is the room rotating, it is rotating I think, beginning to… 'Because any arrangement that you think I might have agreed to concerning our brothers, you and Sensible James and John Thorpe / and I…'

IZ. 'You mean the agreement you suggested and I consented to back when we were wrapped in the same blanket a number of scenes and over a week ago now, in which we would secure each other's brothers…'

A moment between them. HEN *is dancing closer.*

IZ *and* CATH *are obliged to dance away from each other and* CATH *and* HEN *towards each other.* CATH *and* HEN *have both had a bit more to drink.*

HEN. 'You know, one of the things I like about you most, Cath, is that you are so innocent to the world's ills. And when I am with you I feel that I am returned, however temporarily, to that state too…'

CATH. 'You are not so very much older than me, Henry Tilney – '

HEN. 'But in terms of experience.'

CATH. 'Experience?'

HEN. 'Because I have experienced a great deal more than most have at my age.'

CATH. 'Oh, have you, Henry Tilney? You have been in love many times before I expect – '

HEN. 'No. That is not what I meant at all.

Because I do want to.

Because my experiences, such as they have been, both good and unfortunately bad, have gifted me with an understanding of the world that those that have not had such experiences cannot hope to have.'

CATH. 'And what are those experiences Henry Tilney? What is it that weighs so very heavily on your young shoulders?'

HEN. 'There are things.

Confidential family matters which I cannot.

You, for example, an naive and innocent girl from the country, like I say, have not practised many heartaches.'

CATH. 'Heartaches.'

CATH *looks at* IZ, IZ *looks back, they are all still dancing.*

The room is spinning faster and faster. Because in this part you need to show your… There needs to be a demonstration of why the romantic heroine stops dancing with everyone, as is the custom and in this moment chooses to dance with just one man. This man. You. Forever. (*Returning to the script.*) 'Only the normal heartaches and hardships and difficulties of a girl growing into being the heroine she knows herself to be destined to be.'

HEN. 'Ah-ha. And as I say I expect that you read romantic fictions which encourage you to think of yourself this way.'

CATH. 'Why, yes.'

HEN. 'But what about the truth?'

CATH. 'Truth?'

HEN. 'The truth of what really happens. Of what is said and done. Just as an example, what about how true... companionship is formed.'

CATH. 'Companionship? I think that my novels will reveal more about real romance than any dull account of what is supposed to have happened.'

HEN. '*Your* novels?'

CATH (*surprised, that last bit just popped out*). 'Yes.

I am more than a mere novel-reader, Henry.

You must know by now, I am the writer.'

CATH *leans over and vomits*.

Scene Three

The pavement outside the ball. CATH *is bent over, throwing up into the gutter.* IZ *is holding back her hair. The muffled sound of music still pumping through thick Bath walls.* CATH *unbends unsteadily. They are both quite drunk, but* CATH *more so than* IZ.

IZ. 'So you are saying that he... Your preferred suitor is Henry Tilney now and you are insisting that... You pretend that you do not remember our agreement.'

CATH. 'No I...

I do not pretend.'

But time seemed to act so strangely that evening. 'Time seems to spin forward, unspool and then is wound back again. Like cotton on a bobbin.'

IZ. '*Cath.*'

CATH. I felt that that whole evening. 'Like it is not playing by the normal rules.'

CATH *has to steady herself.*

'Because you could still marry my brother, couldn't you?'

IZ *tries to object.*

No. Because you could have, Iz. You could have married my brother. And then we could have visited each other all the time, just as we planned, without there being any suggestion of anything… improper.

(*To audience.*) And so we are obliged to once again spool forward. And in that time that followed –

IZ. Improper? Like that night you mean, after that dancing. After I held your hair back whilst you leant over that gutter. The night before that morning, and all those mornings when it was just the two of us in your bedchamber –

CATH. Iz, don't –

IZ. In your bed.

CATH (*to audience*). And so we are obliged to once again spool forward. And in that time that followed after that important mid-season ball, so much has happened. And what has happened was so much for the better and also, most unfortunately, for the worst.

(*To* IZ.) Because you might be the kind of woman who knows she could never love a man. But.

'Because there is nothing in this world that would allow two women to be… and if I think I could be happy with a husband. Why would you want… Why would you want me to be any less… Any less happy than I might be?'

IZ. 'I am not the one set on making anyone unhappy. Because
I had plans too, to marry well to some inoffensive man who
had money enough to grant me some freedoms. And I was
willing to be content with that. So meeting you has broken
things for me too.

And if you are to go ahead with this marriage to Henry I will
be what then? If I am still to honour my side. To marry your
brother for you. So you can keep coming to the same
bedchambers, lay your head in my lap still, and then lay with
him. And you have that happiness with him too, both those
happinesses.' And you thought that would be… 'You think
I will consent to that. Do you?'

Beat.

'That I would do that for the sake of a greedy girl who wants
to eat all of the cake.'

CATH. Let us spool forward. Let us start with those side of the
scales marked 'the better'. Let me say that after mid-season
ball he… Henry Tilney most chivalrously offered to
accompany me to our lodgings after the dancing. And
stepping outside, into the street, and quite recklessly he
pulled me into a dark recess, and his heart in my chest we…
that is Henry Tilney and I… kissed. My first-ever kiss.

IZ. Can you imagine?

CATH. And now I must turn to the side of the scales labelled
'the worst'.

My new acquaintance who I most rashly named previously
as my most bosom best friend for life.

CATH *and* IZ. The quickness of that female friendship turned
out to be very ill advised. As is so often the case with
feminine attachments formed by romantical young heroines
in unfamiliar towns.

CATH. Last night we heard that she and her brother had quit Bath
altogether and gone back to London. Perhaps… I fancy…
maybe she could have learned that our brother Sensible James

does not have a… sufficient enough income that she would seriously consider any proposal of marriage. Because we did establish she was motivated by money in a most unladylike manner in the very first scene we met her so… that would be… After Isabella found out this important information, she was heard to say that she had no reason for staying. Although not formally engaged it must have been a great blow to my brother, who could not have suspected that the object of his affections would be so moved by money. Miss Isabella Thorpe is a person who I barely recognise and cannot understand.

IZ *leaves the play.*

Scene Four

An Invitation

CATH. And so this brings us to…

HEN *prompts…*

HEN. Mr and Mrs Allan in their lodgings…

CATH. And it will also at last and finally bring us to our title act.

HEN *takes up position as* MR ALLAN, CATH *as* MRS ALLAN. CATH *is still struggling with* IZ's *departure.* HEN *prompts again.*

HEN. But to begin, Mrs Allan is trying to talk to Mr Allan about our heroine.

CATH/MRS ALLAN. '…Dear…?'

HEN. Only Mr Allan will not look up from his paper.

CATH/MRS ALLAN. '…Because, well, the crash must have been terrible upsetting for her. And then that business with her friend leaving Bath in such a hurry.'

Beat.

'Because naturally she was grieved by that too.'

Beat.

'That is only natural.'

HEN/MR ALLAN. 'And then there are her dreams.'

CATH/MRS ALLAN. 'Her... dreams...'

HEN/MR ALLAN. 'I have heard her whimpering in the night.'

CATH/MRS ALLAN. 'So I only hope that the Tilneys...'

HEN/MR ALLAN. 'The Tilneys?'

HEN/MRS ALLAN. 'Yes, dear, that is what I am trying to tell you, our Cath has been, like I said, very down for a great number of reasons.'

HEN/MR ALLAN. 'A great very many heartaches you might say.'

CATH/MRS ALLAN. 'Quite so.' But the point is: 'Because when Henry Tilney called for her this morning she smiled properly for the first time in a long time. Indeed when Mr Tilney offered her his arm she seemed to positively beam.'

HEN/MR ALLAN. 'Well, that is...'

CATH/MRS ALLAN. 'Indeed I do think that Cath is hoping that...'

HEN/MR ALLAN. '...That what?'

CATH/MRS ALLAN (*simultaneous*). 'Well...'

HEN (*simultaneous*). But Mrs Allan does not respond to this...

Because when you have been companions for as long as Mr and Mrs Allan, all that is needed is a slight tilt of the head.

CATH/MRS ALLAN *tilts her head.*

A significant look.

CATH/MRS ALLAN *does a significant look.*

HEN/MR ALLAN. 'Oh.

I see.'

Beat.

'Well, he does seem like a very… companionable young man.'

CATH/MRS ALLAN. 'Oh I can assure you she is quite taken with him, / Mr Allan.'

HEN/MR ALLAN. 'I can see that they could suit each other very… well.'

Beat.

'I suppose while we are here in Bath we are in a kind of *loco parentis*.'

CATH/MRS ALLAN. 'Oh yes! Quite so!'

HEN/MR ALLAN. 'And so it is our responsibility to advise Cath as best we can, in the absence of her actual blood relations, I mean.'

CATH/MRS ALLAN. 'Indeed!'

HEN/MR ALLAN. 'And support her. Because we have known her since the morning after her mam gave birth and having no children of our own we do feel that we do have a parental role in her life.'

CATH/MRS ALLAN. 'Yes, indeed!'

HEN/MR ALLAN. 'And because we see her this way, we do also see her clearly, I think. Including her faults. Because, caught up in her world of fantasy, she does not always see the world as it is, does she?'

Beat.

CATH/MRS ALLAN. 'Oh… well…'

Beat.

HEN/MR ALLAN. 'They are landed, you know. The Tilneys can trace themselves back to some king or another, I believe.'

CATH/MRS ALLAN. 'Oh the titles you mean.'

CATH/MRS ALLAN *looks confused,* HEN/MR ALLAN
elaborates.

HEN/MR ALLAN. 'And that sort of family, however…
well-suited a match might appear to be… when it is
concerning itself with its future it does… Look to other
family trees. To see if they are the right sort of family, the
right sort of tree with the right sort of, well, branches.

So the path towards perfect happiness might not be as clear
as we might… we might hope…

Are you listening to me, dear, because I am not sure that
you, you – '

CATH. But before Aunt Allan could reply, our heroine – That is
to say I, burst in and:

CATH *rises or moves to speak her own line, she holds
a letter.*

'Aunt Allan, Uncle Allan. I have the most wonderful news.
Henry Tilney has invited me to his home! The most wonderful
terrible haunted-sounding place that has been in their family
for many many many generations, an ancestral estate where
I will begin a new chapter in my life and have the most
wonderful tragical haunting gothical adventures. I am going to
go to Northanger Abbey at last!'

ACT FOUR

Scene One

The Arrival

CATH. And so. Act Three. As Katerina de Morland will round
the final corner on the narrow road close to the cliff, she will
look down into a thin mist. Nestled between two pine forests,
quite Austrian in appearance and with dark birds circling its
turreted rooves. 'So,' she will think to herself. 'This is it.'
And a shudder will shiver down her spine.

CATH *has been so carried away by what she has been
saying that she has not noticed that she has arrived. The
sound of horses and carriage pulling away make her jump
slightly.*

She will push open a large wooden door...

CREEEAKKKKKKKKKK!

*A shadow falls across the stage/*CATH.

The shadow flits away.	HEN/ELLIE *appears behind* CATH, *she is holding a bucket and does not look very spooky at all.*	HEN/ELLIE *(from behind* CATH*).* 'I left the door open.'

CATH. 'Oh, Eleanor!' (*To audience*.) Henry's sister.

HEN/ELLIE. 'Left it open quite on purpose so that you could
show yourself in...'

CATH. 'You seemed to appear from nowhere!'

HEN/ELLIE. 'Just as you have!

CATH. 'Out of thin air.'

HEN/ELLIE. 'I am afraid that my father and brother have gone to bed.'

CATH. 'But then they are / not.'

HEN/ELLIE. 'No…'

CATH. 'They are not here to greet me?'

HEN/ELLIE. 'Well, it is a latish hour, Cath.'

CATH. 'Oh.'

HEN/ELLIE. 'May I call you Cath?'

CATH. 'But then who was up – (*Indicating*.) there?'

HEN/ELLIE. 'Up where?'

CATH (*indicating*). 'Up there. Just now. Gliding along the grand gallery that runs all the way around the very top of this most finely appointed, deeply shadowed entrance hall?

Was it you?'

HEN/ELLIE. 'How could it have been?'

CATH. 'Then – '

HEN/ELLIE. 'How could it have been me when I am down here?'

CATH. 'Then who could it have been?'

HEN/ELLIE. 'Down here speaking with you, that would be quite…'

CATH (*simultaneous*). '…impossible…'

HEN/ELLIE (*simultaneous*). '…impossible…'

CATH. And so in this moment this sister's words will trail off and her eyes will be drawn irresistibly upwards, once more, as if against her own will, towards that same grand gallery where she will have just denied anyone could have been.

HEN/ELLIE. 'Shall I show you to your room?'

Scene Two

Buckets / A Locked Trunk

CATH *is surprised at the speed at which they have come to this new room / are in this new scene.* HEN/ELLIE *still has her bucket.*

CATH. 'Oh it is – '

HEN/ELLIE. 'I hope you will be very…'

CATH. 'It looks exceedingly…'

HEN/ELLIE (*simultaneous*). 'Comfortable.'

CATH (*disappointed, simultaneous*). 'Comfortable.'

HEN/ELLIE. 'It is normally my room.'

CATH. 'Oh, I would not want you / to…'

HEN/ELLIE. 'Because you will have noticed that the older part of the abbey has not had attention for a number / of…'

CATH. 'Because I would be very happy to be sequestered to any draughty and cobwebbed nook you might hope to store me away / in…'

HEN/ELLIE. 'Because you will have seen the buckets as we…'

CATH. 'Buckets?'

HEN/ELLIE (*holding up the bucket*). 'Buckets. Catching the water from the rooves. Those pitched rooves…'

CATH. '…With all those lovely battlements…'

HEN/ELLIE. '…that might look quite romantic from the outside, but which do leak. Because I can assure you it is quite a trial to be constantly dripped upon!'

CATH. 'Oh I can assure you I know only too well about the trials of being dripped upon. But I would not have expected that in this great place one would have to endure such… common indignities.'

HEN/ELLIE. 'Would you not? How strange. And yet the ingress of water after a storm is not likely to be any different here than in any other place.'

CATH. 'Well... no. I suppose not...'

HEN/ELLIE. 'In any case, you will find this room is almost completely watertight. And the bed is, as I say, comfortable enough. I am obliged always to let guests sleep here whensoever they visit. Although sadly that has not, as my brother will no doubt have told you, been very often in recent years.'

CATH. 'No, he...'

HEN/ELLIE. 'Since recent events...'

CATH. 'He didn't divulge anything of that nature...'

HEN/ELLIE. 'Did he not? How strange. Your becoming so very close I would have expected he would have wanted to tell you about...

But then. Well. In any case you are my brother's good friend and we are pleased to have you come and I am sure I am very glad to be turned out of my room.

For our most welcomed guest's comfort.'

Beat.

CATH. Because Katerina finds herself afraid to press the issue, but: 'You were not abed when I arrived. And it is a very late hour as you say. So perhaps... maybe you are not able to rest well in / this place?'

HEN/ELLIE. 'No.

I assure you it is. As I say. All quite quite comfortable.'

CATH. 'Unless...

Unless there was something...

Perhaps if there was something uncanny that might disturb your slumber.'

HEN/ELLIE (*amused*). 'Oh well, I don't know about that…'

Beat.

CATH. 'It must be strange, to be awake at night when all are asleep.'

HEN/ELLIE. 'Oh no. It is quite.

It gives me an opportunity to check on all the…'

HEN/ELLIE (*simultaneous*). 'Buckets.'

CATH (*simultaneous*). 'Battlements?'

HEN/ELLIE (*amused*). 'In any case I am quite used to being alone at night, my father and brother are often away. But the servants are always here and I am content enough.'

CATH. 'The figure who I did, as I say, see on the balcony above the entrance hall, their shadow falling briefly across me before they flitted away again, did not look like a servant.'

HEN/ELLIE. 'As I said I think you must be mistaken. No one could have been up there.'

CATH. 'Oh?'

HEN/ELLIE. 'The doors at both ends are locked.'

CATH. 'Well, that is…'

HEN/ELLIE. 'That part of the house is all shut up and no doubt cobwebbed, as you describe, from disuse, and the whole household are asleep, as I said.'

CATH. And a third shudder. The first being in the carriage on seeing the abbey for the first time, the second when this sister denied that shadowy figure that flitted across that balcony, so this is the third shudder which will be sent down our heroine's spine on hearing this news of that shut-up suite of rooms. And in this moment our heroine's keen eyes will alight upon…

A trunk appears.

'Oh. But what about this trunk?'

HEN/ELLIE. 'Oh that, I had forgotten that was… that that was… It is, that is to say that, like so much in this house it is impossible to say how many generations it has been here. How it first came to be put in this room I know not, but, I have not had it moved, because I thought it might sometimes be of some use in holding hats… or bonnets…'

CATH *makes to move towards the trunk.*

(*Quickly.*) 'The worst of it is that it is quite impossible to open.'

CATH *takes the hint,* HEN/ELLIE *relaxes.*

'We lost the key some time ago. However, at least in that corner it is out of your way. Well. You have had a long journey and I expect you will want to unpack and make yourself as… comfortable as you can be. I will leave you to…'

HEN/ELLIE *vanishes.*

Scene Three

An Echoing Chamber

Candlelight.

CATH *is in bed.*

Wind. The spooky kind.

CATH. And so we will find our heroine in bed.

HEN. In bed, but in common with the handful of nights that proceeded this night, when she was still in Bath…

CATH. The wind will roar down the great chimney.

HEN.…resisting sleep.

CATH. Rain will beat at the long uncurtained windows. The wind will rattle about crumbling stone walls.

HEN. Then suddenly drops.

Wind drops.

CATH. And our heroine's ears will start to detect a whispering.

Whispering.

Beat.

'...Isabella?'

HEN. 'My sister says that Catherine Morland was asking questions.'

CATH. A voice she will know...

...she will know instantly and unmistakably, as that of her most romantical...

HEN. 'Questions about why we did not stay up and meet her carriage.'

CATH. It will be the voice of her most romantical hero, Henry Tilney of Northanger Abbey, of course, who is meant to be abed. And on hearing her own name mentioned, our romantic heroine will not be able to resist slipping out from between her cold sheets. And she will hear another deeper voice rising to meet Henry's.

HEN/GENERAL TILNEY. 'Well, that is good... It is good we have put her on her mettle. Because she must not think that you receive her too keenly, Henry...'

HEN (*as himself*). '...And furthermore, Father, she was asking about the buildings.'

HEN/GENERAL TILNEY. 'I am sure she was. A girl like that. Wanting to know the cost of everything and understanding the value of nothing.'

HEN. 'No, Father, you misunderstand my meaning. The gallery that runs around the top of the entrance hall.'

CATH. And for a moment there will be nothing. Only the sound of the whistling wind again, as it whips around long-deserted corridors. And Katerina will think she could almost have, she could almost have fancied she imagined this conversation but then...

HEN. 'And which has doors leading to...

To those rooms.

Eleanor told her they are locked up of course, but...'

HEN/GENERAL TILNEY. 'But?'

HEN. 'But Catherine is quite the most curious young woman I have ever met. And I think she will... I do think she will begin to come to some sort of... understanding of what has gone on.'

CATH. And your heroine will creep even closer to the door of her room.

HEN. Squatting. Her small ear pressed to the very keyhole.

CATH. So I will be able to hear when your father asks...

HEN/GENERAL TILNEY. 'But you like the girl?'

HEN (*as himself*). 'I. Well. Like I have said she is curious and wilful and funny. I don't know if she always knows she is. But she is funny. And I do think underneath her fancifulness. I believe her to have a good heart.'

CATH. And the voices will...

HEN. They seem to fade away again, at last.

CATH. But one more comment will reach the ear of our listener

HEN/GENERAL TILNEY. 'You must make a good match, Henry.

We must not let anything. Anything or anyone get in the way of that!'

CATH. And in this moment a chill wind will whip round and up Katerina's thin white chemise as her eyes will alight once again on that trunk.

The trunk appears again.

HEN. That trunk that my sister went to great lengths to warn Catherine off...

CATH. ...the younger sister who might have seemed so welcoming but who was concerned to make sure that

Katerina did not open up anything that might have... And because all this, everything that she will have experienced in this place since her arrival late at night in the middle of a storm, will seem to speak of the sublime terror of a secret locked up, but now it will seem...

HEN. To our most wilful and impetuous heroine...

CATH....Clamouring, to be opened...

HEN. With trembling fingers, she feels that it is not locked.

CATH....With difficulty, for something...

HEN. Perhaps her own conscience.

CATH....Will still seem to resist her efforts.

Another CREAKKKKKKKKKKK...

Her quick eyes will fall directly on a roll of paper pushed back into the furthest recess of the cavity.

Apparently for concealment.

CATH *seizes a rolled-up sheaf of paper.*

HEN. Half a glance suffice to ascertain written characters, and she is about to read what she was / never meant to see...

A sudden knocking.

CATH *turns in surprise.*

The candle is snuffed out. Darkness.

The knocking stops.

In darkness:

CATH. She will retreat to her bed.

HEN. Hollow murmurs seem to creep along the locked-up gallery once again. And as she falls into a fitful sleep and her blood chills by the sound of distant weeping and words half-remembered, held within the echoing chamber of her own chest, and if we listened at *her* keyhole we would hear a faint whimpering coming from that lonely room...

Scene Four

Hyacinths

HEN. But at breakfast all appears quite normal.

CATH. 'I was awake for a time.'

HEN. My father having just enquired about how Catherine has slept.

CATH. And Katerina having replied, all will fall silent once again.

Beat.

'The wind does whistle so magnificently about the abbey.'

Beat.

'In any case we have a charming morning for it.'

Our heroine will smile round.

HEN. All stare back at her.

CATH. And still fingering the tightly rolled scroll of paper in her pocket, which she discovered in that trunk, but will not yet have dared to read. 'What beautiful hyacinths! I have just learned to love a hyacinth.'

HEN/GENERAL TILNEY. 'And how might you learn?'

CATH. 'I… Sorry?'

HEN/GENERAL TILNEY. 'By accident or argument?'

(*As himself.*) 'Father.'

CATH. 'Neither. That is. My Aunt Allan used to take great pains, year after year, to make me like hyacinths; but I never could, till I saw them the other day in Bath; they were the same flowers and yet, somehow, in their new surrounding, quite different.'

HEN/GENERAL TILNEY. 'Ah-ha. Well. A taste for flowers is always desirable in your sex as a means of enticement in getting you out of doors.'

CATH. 'Oh, but I do not need any such enticement, the pleasure of walking and breathing in fresh air is quite enough for me, General…'

HEN/GENERAL TILNEY. 'I see…'

CATH. 'Indeed before going to Bath I was out more than half my time. Indeed my mam said I was never within!'

HEN/GENERAL TILNEY. '"My mam" indeed, Henry!'

Beat.

CATH. 'That is. I mean to say. I like to walk sometimes…'

HEN/GENERAL TILNEY. 'Ah yes and I suppose the habit remains unchanged despite your new surroundings.'

(*As himself.*) 'Father, please…'

CATH. 'I had thought that I might meet Mrs Tilney this morning…' A clatter of cutlery. General Tilney, Henry Tilney and even little Eleanor, who will have contrived to make herself as small and as still to this point as possible. All will fall suddenly and completely silent. '…At breakfast.'

HEN/GENERAL TILNEY. 'I must ride again today, Henry.'

CATH. 'I should so like to meet her?'

HEN/GENERAL TILNEY. 'To London. I have received another missive which… As you know my previous enquiries on your behalf were frustratingly inconclusive. But I am hopeful that I will have that conclusive answer tonight for you and that will be a conclusion to all things one way or the other.'

CATH. But Katerina will not be listening to these words. Instead she will be staring up at the great many oils of all the Tilneys' great and noble ancestors, hung about the large and great dining hall.

HEN. And above General Tilney's head…

CATH. At the head of the table…

HEN. A large light square on an otherwise dark interior…

CATH. Where the largest oil must have previously been hung. But now quite empty.

Scene Five

Gloaming

HEN. 'So. You have seen the market gardens…'

CATH. '…Yes…'

HEN. 'And the rose gardens, and the shrubbery. And you have professed to have found all of it most fascinating.'

CATH (*as if it is not*). 'Oh yes, most fascinating.'

HEN. Even if she did look quite bored. 'And finally, over here are the hothouses.'

Beat.

'Where we force things that should not grow in this climate.'

CATH. 'I see. Yes, and it is all very… Most distracting indeed. But I have lost my bearings. Which way were the forests that I passed through when I arrived in my carriage?'

HEN. 'Forests?'

CATH. 'The forests I looked down through. (*A little impatiently.*) Pines. Quite Austrian.'

HEN. 'Oh, well there are trees and…'

CATH. 'Is it this way?'

Beat.

HEN. 'It is easy, is it not, in a new landscape to find oneself disoriented.'

CATH. 'Well, yes.'

HEN. 'To feel that one has lost one's bearings and without a guide or map.'

CATH. '…Exactly…'

HEN. 'You can feel… Because sometimes even familiar well-worn paths. Paths you thought you would walk with… enthusiasm can be made to seem strange…'

CATH. '…Strange?'

HEN. 'Strange or ill-advised. Because of what you have come to know of the world.'

Beat.

'What you have come to know of the world or who you have discovered yourself to be in it.

And do you know what that feels like? Because I think you do a little. Cath. And I think we have that in common. Even if the reasons are quite different. That feeling of not being suited to the path we are meant to walk, simply on account of what we have experienced in this world… or who we have come to know ourselves to be in it.'

Beat.

'Are you all right, because you don't look quite well.'

CATH (*pulling herself together*). 'Because I saw old pine trees and I would like to walk that long and winding and, yes, well-worn path I saw which must go right through. But I would be afraid to do so on my own. It would only be possible with someone to provide protection…'

HEN. 'A friend.'

CATH. But, before they will be able to set off down that path. She and he. In the gloaming.

HEN. In this moment, Cath happens to glance up. And in one of the great lancet windows, the shadow of General Tilney.

IZ *appears up high, silhouetted.*

He must have returned from London in the intervening hours. And outlined in a cursive window which would more naturally frame the face of some great and ancient wrinkled monk. In the almost-extinguished evening light. Lit from underneath his features look quite…

CATH.…Different.

HEN. Cath ventures a wave.

CATH *waves.*

CATH. As he will stare down. Unsmiling.

CATH *drops her hand when there is no returning wave.*

IZ/GENERAL TILNEY *leaves his place high up and we can hear him stamping quickly down an unseen flight of stairs through the following.*

IZ/JOHN THORPE *is drunk.*

IZ/JOHN THORPE. 'AHHHHHHH it is the General.'

CATH. And there will be something in the turn of his features which will speak of him not having behaved altogether well.

IZ. Because a chorus of 'General, General, General'… had gone up round the grubby back room of the grimy drinking establishment at the appointed hour that afternoon.

CATH. And our heroine will realise with a jolt that she does not altogether trust him.

HEN. 'We should go back inside now. My father will want to talk to me about these enquiries which I suspect he has at last satisfied himself in and I expect you will want to get dressed for dinner.'

IZ/GENERAL TILNEY. 'I got your letter and I came.'

CATH. I thought you'd left my story…

IZ. 'Left it.'

HEN. 'I know how much you care about behaving with the correct decorum. And my father does expect us to / dress for dinner here…'

CATH. I thought you'd gone.

IZ/JOHN THORPE. 'I summoned you. Can you imagine, me, John Thorpe…'

IZ/GENERAL TILNEY. 'You said that you had information.'

IZ/JOHN THORPE. 'I do. A great deal of information pertaining to interests or, rather, that is an interest, that we share.'

CATH (*to the audience*). This is not part of the.

IZ/GENERAL TILNEY. 'You explained in this... letter of yours.'

IZ/JOHN THORPE. 'Yes.'

A moment between CATH *and* IZ. IZ *decides to carry on...*

'So I will cut to it: Your son and heir, Henry Tilney. The lover of muslins and constant moping. Enough to make any room heavy with his limp-wristed sadness. He is... This interest. Your son's prospect. She is not what she seems.'

CATH. No...

IZ. And in slurred words and graphic gesticulations he... That is to say my brother, John Thorpe, said to General Tilney, that afternoon, what he had learnt about you. All of it.

CATH. All of it?!

IZ/JOHN THORPE. 'And for my part I could not be more pleased that my engagement with Catherine Morland was called off. Because to be married to a girl like that. But for my Izzy...'

And because to have betrayed everything that went on between us two...

All of it. Cath.

CATH. I...

IZ. 'Well.' My brother said to General Tilney that afternoon. 'For my sister. Because I might not always have been a good brother. Or a worthy chaperone. But even an irredeemable rogue can love his sister, can't he? John Thorpe is capable of that. And it now seems as if the marriage to Catherine Morland's brother was Izzy's only route to happiness.'

And once again my brother sent round another round of: 'General General General.' Because we are approaching the final turning of this story, Cath. And this scene, that you intended to stay offstage and out of the reach of our audience in a grubby back room of a pub in a less salubrious part of London. The whole final turning of this story revolves in this moment around these two men. Not any of us.

Scene Six

An Echoing Chamber (Again)

CATH *wrestles back control.*

IZ. General Tilney will not be at dinner. And the mealtime conversation between Eleanor, Henry and Cath will be somewhat strained. Somewhat closed off. As if there is something…

CATH.…yes, being left unsaid…

IZ. Consequentially Cath will slip off to bed. And between the cold sheets of the bed again. And our heroine. Because exhausted as she is by now, she can resist the dreams.

CATH. The dream of a dream.

IZ. She has been pushing away to this point no more.

CATH. The curtainless windows. The moaning only increases. And once again the handle of the door will start to rattle and shake as the moaning will only get louder and louder.

IZ. A keening, wailing sort of noise.

CATH. So loud that it will become a kind of silence.

IZ. And into that great unbearable absence that follows. What my Cath had been dreading most.

CATH. You…

IZ. I…

In the dark:

'Are you awake?'

IZ *is in* CATH*'s bed with her.*

'You were turning about…'

CATH. 'I had a dream. I was in the garden at the vicarage and everyone was there. Sensible James, Nigel, and the rest of my brothers. Mam and Pa. The Allans. I was standing under the cherry trees, which I always thought were so unremarkable, and you were standing opposite me. And Father was wearing his collar.'

IZ. It was a strange dream. Because there was a circle of other people in strange clothes. They were all watching us. The sun was very bright overhead and there was birdsong but it was all a bit too...

CATH. 'A little too bright, a little too artificial, and then Father said something. And then you were saying something back and it was something like...'

CATH *and* IZ. 'Friends, in the fear of the Lord, and before this assembly, I take my friend to be my...'

IZ. 'Promising, through divine assistance...'

CATH. '...to be unto her a loving and faithful...'

CATH *and* IZ. '...until it shall please the Lord by death to separate us...'

CATH. 'And then a great falling of petals around us.'

IZ. And you giggled into me.

CATH. Our legs entwined, and pushed up against me...
I imagined... because I did imagine in that moment our union, Izzy...

IZ. But then your aunt stirred in the next room. The noise of the Bath street outside. And then the cold sheets again, the curtainless windows.

All contrived to remind you that...

IZ *pushes* CATH *away.*

CATH. Our heroine. Cold sheets. Curtainless windows. Moaning without words. Words. Silence and the horror of it. And still the locked chest. And on waking with a jolt in the middle of the night and the handle of the door rattling once again, Katerina de Morland will make the decision once and for all to discover what this is all about. She will slip out of the bed and out of the room and along the corridor. She will find herself in front of the locked door that leads to the locked-up gallery.

Because what Henry hinted at at that mid-season ball. The tensions at breakfast and the strange comments he made in the too-too-perfect gardens and General Tilney's absence that followed at dinner. The scroll of paper that she will still be clutching, clutching close between fingers yet unable to unfurl and read. And above all the absent unspoken mother and the daughter eager to keep the secrets of that haunted home locked up. As the handle of the door will start to turn. The existence of true wickedness and the whole family now willing to pretend that it does not. I could never have hoped to fall so completely into a true gothic. As I will open my innocent virgin mouth to [scream]...

Scene Seven

A Secret Revealed

HEN. 'Good God!'

CATH. 'Mr Tilney!'

HEN. 'Catherine!'

CATH. 'How came you here?'

HEN. 'How came I? Why should I not come this way? In my own home. And may I not, in my turn, ask how *you* came here? At so late an hour.'

CATH. 'I have come to see.'

   Beat.

   (*Dramatically.*) '...Your mother's rooms.'

HEN. 'My mother's rooms?'

CATH. 'You do not deny it then?'

HEN. 'Why would I? And can I ask, did my sister leave you to find your way into all the rooms in the house in this manner?'

CATH. 'Well, no she... shewed me over the... Some of the less remarkable parts of the house on my arrival.'

HEN. 'But tonight she sent you to look at these parts I suppose? Altogether alone?'

Beat.

'My mother's rooms are very commodious, are they not?'

CATH. 'Your sister said that they were shut up and cobwebbed from disuse.'

HEN. 'Large and cheerful-looking and the dressing closets so well disposed.'

CATH. 'Along with a trunk in my room which she said was locked. Inside there was a rolled-up sheaf of paper that, I will find it here.'

CATH *thrusts the sheaf of paper into* HEN's *hands.*

HEN (*reading*). 'Two ribbons (red and pink), pale-blue muslins, three of thirty inches a piece. A small box of caraway biscuits.'

CATH....

HEN. 'A shopping list in my mother's hand.'

CATH. 'So all her things are here and I saw... I know that I saw something flitting across. Or rather someone. But your sister insisted. She insisted I was mistaken. And you. You let me believe, all of you did at breakfast, that she did not live here. Why are you, why are you all keeping her – '

HEN. 'I am not keeping... No one is keeping her from you. She has not been locked up within the walls of her own house. I had thought someone as curious as you and who prides themselves on possessing so great an imagination should have worked out the truth of it by now.'

CATH. 'Indeed, I think I have because I believed and now am confirmed that there is some mischief. Some terrible wickedness has befallen her.'

HEN. 'Indeed. She is dead, Catherine. My mother died only three months ago.'

Beat.

CATH. 'Well. But. Indeed.'

Beat.

'Because then I, indeed…

Then you…

Because you kept this tragical… This quite tragical information. You and your family have made her death a secret from me and from the world I think.'

HEN. 'The Allans knew and most of our friends in Bath.'

CATH. 'And I wonder. I cannot help but wonder…'

HEN. 'It was only you that was not told.'

CATH. 'Because you were…'

HEN. 'My father believed that it might put any match off. And I. Well. I did want to tell you, Cath, but…'

CATH. 'Because I might guess that you were at university when this tragical event happened so when your mother passed it was only your sister… your quite defenceless young sister…'

HEN. 'I came home as soon as Eleanor wrote to me but I did not…'

CATH. 'And your father…'

HEN. 'It is to my eternal regret that I did not arrive in time.'

CATH. 'And I see now I should have been more attentive to your obvious pain. Your absences in those first few weeks of our acquaintance both physical and constitutional. But. I would not be able to forgive myself now if I did not ask, was no one else with them when your mother… passed?'

HEN. 'My mother's illness was… A constitutional palsy she had suffered from her entire life. So although the final seizure did, yes, come suddenly, it was not altogether unexpected. It was, to some extent, to be anticipated. So you see. No mystery. No tragedy, only a great weight of sadness, as you say, on all my family's shoulders.

But the domestic unpretending merits of a person who enjoyed to walk between tall trees on her better days, who would prefer caraway biscuits over any other sort. Could eat a whole box in a single sitting. The kind of person an imperfect man such as my father could love his whole life. She is not the sort of character that would ever appear in your kinds of fictions and so you have created... From these circumstances you infer some probability of negligence on the part of my father, is it? Or it may be, something less pardonable.'

Beat.

'My father has brought news from London which... He met a young man by the name of John Thorpe.'

CATH. 'Oh.'

HEN. 'John Thorpe had written to Father. A quite appalling letter exposing you. You and who you are. He has established via John Thorpe that you are no blood relation of the Allans.'

Beat.

CATH. 'Well no.'

HEN. 'And that you are from an even poorer and less well-established family than he had thought. That you are quite destitute.'

CATH. 'Oh no, we are only not rich.'

HEN. 'So consequentially my father does not think that it is appropriate that you and I...

That you should stay in this house beyond tonight.

Because he is, as I say. He was. An imperfect husband. He is an imperfect father. An imperfect man. And he has decided that you are no longer.

And I had thought to fight him on these matters, knowing that you are indeed only genteelly poor.'

Because you did. Despite your faults. Your faults which you have allowed us to display in all there. Because during that time we have also, I think, demonstrated how your friendship allowed me some brief. Distraction. From the sadness I felt so very...

And because I once heard it said that friendship was certainly the finest balm for the pangs of any sort of... disappointed love.

And why shouldn't that friendship have been the basis for a marriage?

CATH. Hen...

HEN. Two people who were both so heartsore. Heartsore and broken by who we could no longer hold. And because, in the end, why shouldn't that have been enough?

CATH. Enough?

HEN. To provide a happy enough ending.

IZ *enters*.

CATH. No. We. That is not...

Because I did betray you, Henry. And it is...

That would not have been enough for me anyway. And it must not be enough for you either.

And because this story of mine must be what really happened... Because *I* once heard it said that the truth of what really happened. Of what was said and done. That is what is important in fictions. A version of it at least. So we shall say... let us have you say that a carriage has been arranged...

HEN *does not want to say the next bit*. IZ *takes some item of clothing from him, and starts to do the final bit for him...*

IZ/HEN. 'A carriage has been arranged, which will deliver you back to the small and humble vicarage in some northern part of the country. And I don't expect that you and I shall ever see each other again.'

HEN. 'So I suppose you have…'

IZ/HEN. 'You have achieved what you set out to.'

CATH. You could say: 'You have created a kind of tragedy.'

IZ/HEN. 'And very romantic it is too.'

HEN. 'You must be very pleased…'

CATH. And as I am about to leave…

IZ. Your heavy cloak perhaps about your neck…

HEN. Your fingers wrapped around the gothic iron handle of the door one last time.

CATH. When you could say those words that finally broke my heroine's heart so completely.

IZ/HEN. 'I do wonder about the writers that you seek so passionately to emulate.'

HEN. 'What normal natural heartaches had they locked up, do you think? What was it that they knew about their own souls that they sought to turn their characters into angels and devils instead?'

Epilogue

The Compression of Pages

CATH. And my audience will sense. You will sense that we are all hastening towards… This is the part where we all must hasten towards that inevitable. Perfect felicity.

HEN. Which means. Perfect happiness.

IZ. The happy ending.

CATH. But first I need to bring back my heroine to her home in solitude and disgrace.

HEN. But a heroine returning to where she began in solitude and disgrace is such a sentimental image.

IZ. Swiftly therefore shall her carriage drive through the northern county of this country.

CATH. There will be no heartbroken face at a rain-misted window.

HEN. The welcome, when she arrives in the small and narrow place she began what felt like a lifetime ago, and which must have been keenly anticipated could instead be modest.

CATH. I will not say how all assembled at the door, to welcome her with affectionate eagerness…

IZ. Her mam in that same apron, with floured hands…

HEN/MAM. 'Oh, our Cath…'

CATH. Her pa and his scratchy moustache on her cheek when he lent down to kiss his only daughter.

IZ/PA. 'Come here, you.'

CATH. Smelling of the smoke from the fire.

HEN. And the sight of all those too-too-numerous brothers.

IZ. How all these senses awakened the best feelings of Cath's heart...

HEN. How she found herself soothed beyond anything that she had believed possible.

CATH. And over the next few days I will not describe how she could neither sit still, nor employ herself for ten minutes together...

IZ. Walking around and around the modest grounds...

HEN. As if nothing but motion was voluntary.

CATH. Remembering and regretting so much of what had happened.

IZ. What she had said and done.

CATH. Those betrayals which were, she now understood, hers alone.

HEN. And some years later...

CATH. I will not describe the final moments of this story when our heroine was visiting a shop in this country's proper capital, how she watched as a female figure, inspecting a new volume.

HEN. This new volume.

CATH. This story. The back of her head and when she turned her face.

IZ. And it was her. Because there she found herself at last, pressed between the pages of a book, just as she had always hoped.

CATH. Or perhaps I will.

IZ. Because here she is under that same cherry tree.

CATH. And she is quite alone.

IZ. But also, not alone at all.

HEN. Because her journals and my papers and all the pamphlets and novels and lists and receipts in her lap.

CATH. And I will say she will start read.

IZ. That our heroine shall not flinch from any of it.

CATH. Because the ending of this story is in its beginning. This place where it started, this unremarkable afternoon when these people who loved me most helped me to start to recall the imperfect felicity of it all.

Petals drop from the cherry tree.

All of it. Where I started to write.

The End.

A Nick Hern Book

This adaptation of *Northanger Abbey* first published in Great Britain in 2024 as a paperback original by Nick Hern Books Limited, The Glasshouse, 49a Goldhawk Road, London W12 8QP, in association with the Orange Tree Theatre, Richmond, Octagon Theatre, Bolton, Stephen Joseph Theatre, Scarborough and Theatre by the Lake, Keswick

This adaptation of *Northanger Abbey* copyright © 2024 Zoe Cooper

Zoe Cooper has asserted her right to be identified as the author of this work

Cover photography by Rebecca Need-Menear

Designed and typeset by Nick Hern Books, London
Printed in Great Britain by Mimeo Ltd, Huntingdon, Cambridgeshire PE29 6XX

A CIP catalogue record for this book is available from the British Library

ISBN 978 1 83904 313 0

www.nickhernbooks.co.uk/environmental-policy